STO

S0-ERS-480

Silver for General Washington

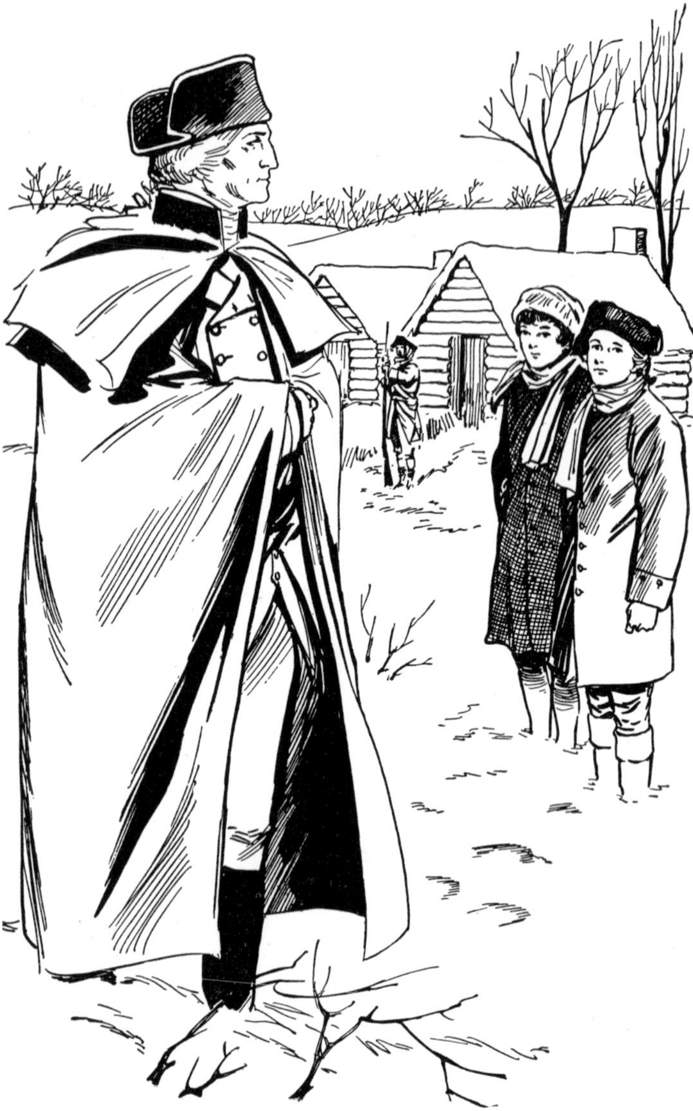

SILVER FOR GENERAL WASHINGTON

A Story of Valley Forge

Enid LaMonte Meadowcroft

ILLUSTRATED BY LEE AMES

THOMAS Y. CROWELL COMPANY

NEW YORK

Books by the Author

THE GIFT OF THE RIVER

BY WAGON AND FLATBOAT

SHIP BOY WITH COLUMBUS

SILVER FOR GENERAL WASHINGTON

THE FIRST YEAR

ON INDIAN TRAILS WITH DANIEL BOONE

BY SECRET RAILWAY

TEXAS STAR

*Copyright © 1957, 1944 by Thomas Y. Crowell Company
All rights reserved. No part of this book may be
reproduced in any form, except by a reviewer,
without the permission of the publisher.*

*Manufactured in the United States of America
by the Vail-Ballou Press, Inc., Binghamton, New York*

LIBRARY OF CONGRESS CATALOG CARD NO. 57-10281

Ninth Printing

To Emeline La Monte Ross

Contents

ONE:	*Bad News*	1
TWO:	*Gil Loses a Letter*	15
THREE:	*Things Begin to Happen*	29
FOUR:	*The Enemy Arrives*	38
FIVE:	*Unwelcome Visitors*	48
SIX:	*"I'll Find a Way"*	60
SEVEN:	*Eleven Thousand Hungry Men*	75
EIGHT:	*Something Strange Afoot*	90
NINE:	*Gil Finds and Loses a Friend*	106
TEN:	*A Daring Plan*	124
ELEVEN:	*Trapping a Spy*	137
TWELVE:	*Ezra Is Frightened*	158
THIRTEEN:	*Escape from Philadelphia*	175
FOURTEEN:	*Valley Forge Again*	195
FIFTEEN:	*Gil and Danny Call on General Washington*	209
SIXTEEN:	*The Army Marches Away*	228

CHAPTER ONE

Bad News

GILBERT EMMET held his candle carefully as he limped across the room and stopped beside the big four-poster bed where his younger sister, Jenifer, lay soundly sleeping.

"Jen, Jen, wake up," he said, leaning down and shaking her gently.

With a little sigh Jenifer turned over and buried her head deeper in the pillows. Then she murmured sleepily, "Go away, Martha. Please go away. It's not time to get up yet."

Gilbert grinned and shook her again. "I'm not Martha," he declared, "and you must wake up this minute. Father wants to see us in his study at once."

"What?" Jenifer sat up, pushed her tumbled brown curls back from her face, and blinked her eyes. "But Gil Emmet, it's the middle of the night," she protested. "What's the matter?"

Silver for General Washington

Her brother shook his head and the red tassel on his nightcap swung back and forth like the pendulum of a clock. "I don't know what's the matter," he replied. "Martha woke me up a minute ago and sent me to get you. She says that the soldier who came while we were at supper has just gone, and Father looks very much worried and wants to see us right away. So come on, Jen. Hurry up."

Gilbert turned and started for the door. Climbing quickly out of bed, Jenifer slipped her dressing robe over her high-necked white bed-gown and followed her brother's bobbing candle down the broad stairway. She was wide awake now, and a little frightened.

"Wait for me, Gil," she whispered, and caught at Gilbert's hand.

The door of Mr. Emmet's study was ajar and the boy and girl entered the room together. At his desk in one corner of the room their father sat writing.

"Sit down, you two, and be as still as you can for a few minutes," he said, hardly looking up from his work.

Jenifer noticed that his hair needed powdering

and that the black ribbon which fastened the little silk bag in which he wore his queue had come untied. At another time she would have fixed it for him at once. But now she perched herself anxiously on the edge of a big elbow-chair near his desk and waited for him to finish his writing.

Silver for General Washington

Gilbert blew out the candle which he carried and set it down on the table. Then he moved a low footstool close to an open window.

The August night was hot and very sultry. No breeze stirred the ruffled white curtains and the only sound in the quiet room was the scratching of Mr. Emmet's goose-quill pen. Outside, however, the air was alive with the steady chatter of katydids and locusts. A bullfrog croaked hoarsely down in the garden pool. In the distance Gil heard the noise of carriage wheels rattling over the cobblestones which paved the streets of Philadelphia, and the town crier calling the hour. "Past midnight and another hot morning."

Then from the kitchen at the back of the house came the high-pitched voice of old Martha, the Negro slave, who had taken care of the Emmet children ever since the death of their mother shortly after Jenifer was born. Martha was talking with Ezra, her husband. Gilbert wondered what the two could be doing in the kitchen at such a late hour.

"And what on earth has happened to make Father get us out of bed in the middle of the

Bad News

night?" he asked himself, slapping vigorously at a mosquito which buzzed near his ear.

There was one thing he was sure of, he decided. Whatever had happened, the soldier who had arrived earlier in the evening had had something to do with it. It had been no surprise to him or to Jenifer when an American officer in a buff and blue uniform had called on their father, for they were accustomed to seeing soldiers about the city.

Only two years had passed since the thirteen colonies of North America had begun to fight a long and bitter war against England, their mother country. Although there had been no battles in Philadelphia, the capital of the country, much of the business of the war was carried on there. And all sorts of men had come to the Emmets' comfortable brick house on Chestnut Street to talk with Mr. Emmet.

What his father and these men discussed behind the closed doors of the study Gilbert did not know. Indeed, he did not even have a very clear idea what the war itself was about. But he would never forget the day, a little more than a year before, when the thirteen colonies had declared they were thirteen

Silver for General Washington

states and would no longer be ruled by England. That had been one of the most important days in Gil's life.

In the first place it had been his eleventh birthday, July 8, 1776. In the second place his father had given him what he had wanted more than anything else in the world—a new violin. And in the third place he had fallen out of the cherry tree, breaking his leg so badly that the doctor said he would limp a little for the rest of his life.

He had climbed the tree only so that he might look over the high garden wall into the State House yard, where a crowd of people had gathered to listen to his father's friend, Colonel Nason, read something called a "Declaration of Independence." He remembered well how quietly the men and women had stood in the heat of that July day listening to words which he could not hear.

Then all at once everybody had begun to cheer and cry, "God bless the free States of North America," and he had leaned so far forward to watch them that he had lost his balance, pitched out of the tree, and crashed to the ground below. As he lay there with his leg doubled under him calling

Bad News

for help, all the bells in the city had begun to ring to announce the reading of the Declaration, and it was several minutes before anyone heard his cries.

He made a wry face now as he recalled how long and loudly he had had to shout before any help came and how badly his leg had hurt. So absorbed was he in his memories of the day that he had almost forgotten where he was, and he jumped when his father suddenly pushed back his chair and swung around.

Mr. Emmet smiled. "What's the matter, Gil—dreaming again?" he asked. Then his smile faded and he looked soberly at the children. "Well, young Emmets, I have some news for you."

"Good news?" asked Jenifer hopefully.

"No, it's very bad," Mr. Emmet replied. "I have just received word by a special messenger that the British fleet which left New York in mid-July is is now sailing into Chesapeake Bay. The redcoats will probably attack Philadelphia within the next few days. For that reason I want to get you both out of the city as quickly as possible."

Gilbert looked up, his blue eyes shining. "I'd rather stay right here with you, sir," he declared.

"I'd like to get into the fight if there's going to be one."

"I won't be here, Gil," his father replied. "Only this evening I agreed to go on a journey—one which may keep me away for many months. I am leaving tonight."

"Tonight!" echoed Gil in dismay. "Where are you going?"

"That I can't tell you," his father replied, reaching out to put a strong arm around Jenifer, who had come to stand close beside his chair. "It is an errand I have promised to do for General Washington—a secret errand and perhaps a dangerous one. I shall be better able to accomplish it if I know that you children are safe in the country."

"Dangerous," Jenifer wailed softly. "Oh, Father, I wish you didn't have to go." And she leaned over quickly, pretending to straighten the silver buckle at her father's knee, so that no one could see the tears which had rushed to her eyes. Her voice was muffled as she asked, "Where are you going to send us?"

Mr. Emmet did not answer. Instead he swung

Bad News

his daughter around so that he could look squarely at her.

"See here, young lady, you sound weepy," he declared, giving her a friendly little shake. "That won't do. Remember this, Jen—Emmets don't cry. When they are frightened and unhappy they clench their fists and grin. And the blacker things look the harder they grin." He pulled her down on his knee. "Here, let me tell you what my plan for you is, for I have not much more time to talk."

Making a brave attempt to smile, Jenifer sank back against her father's shoulder, while Gilbert pulled his footstool closer.

"Tomorrow morning as soon as it is light," Mr. Emmet continued, "Ezra will drive you two out to Valley Forge and leave you with Aunt Abigail and Uncle Benjamin Gardner. When he gets back, he and Martha will lock up the house and go at once to stay with their daughter across the river in New Jersey. They will stay there and you will remain with Aunt Abigail until I get home again, no matter how long I am away or what the redcoats do."

Silver for General Washington

"Does Aunt Abigail know we are coming?" Gil asked.

"No, I have had no time to send her word," Mr. Emmet replied. "But I am sure that she will welcome you and take care of you for your mother's sake." He passed his hand lightly over Jen's curls. "I wish I were as sure of your Uncle Benjamin. He's as hot-tempered a man as I have ever known. Well—" He stood up suddenly, setting Jenifer on her feet. "I can see that neither one of you will sleep a wink until after I have left, so there is no use sending you back to bed.

"Jen, you will find Martha upstairs packing your trunk. See if you can't do something to assist her. Gil, you go down cellar and help Ezra dig a good deep hole under the northwest corner of the house. We'll bury all the silver there and any other things which the redcoats might find of value, if they should invade the city. I have one more letter to write and then I will come down and lend you a hand. Run on, now, both of you. Look sharp."

Obediently Jenifer started for the door, but Gil hesitated.

"May I—may I take my violin to Valley

10

Bad News

Forge?" he asked, looking anxiously at his father.

For a moment Mr. Emmet studied the boy's upturned face as though he were learning by heart every curve and freckle. Then he smiled.

"Of course you may take it," he answered. "Take your music too and try to learn that new Handel piece which Mr. Walker brought you from London, so that you can play it for me when I get home."

Gil grinned happily. "I will, sir," he promised, and he limped after Jenifer.

The next few hours were busy ones indeed. Looking back afterwards, Jen declared that they seemed to her almost like a dream—and a muddled dream at that. There was a great deal of scurrying around from one candle-lighted room to another, deciding what should be packed, what must be left behind, and what must be buried in the deep hole which Gil and Ezra were digging in the cellar.

There was a mysterious and exciting moment when Jenifer held a candle high while her father and Ezra lowered into that hole a big chest containing the family silver and several other precious belongings, and then helped Gil tramp the earth

Silver for General Washington

down so that no one should suspect that anything was buried there.

There was a clattering of dishes in the kitchen as Martha prepared a hurried meal for Mr. Emmet, which he ate at the long table in the dining room with the children sitting on either side. And then, almost before they knew it, there was Ezra at the dining room door.

"Your horse am ready, Mr. Emmet," Ezra drawled. "Ah done fixed the saddle bags like you tole me and she am ready to go."

"Thank you, Ezra." Hastily swallowing the last drop of coffee, Mr. Emmet pushed his chair back and stood up. In the hall he picked up two letters which lay on the table and gave them to Gil.

"One of these is for your Aunt Abigail, to explain to her why I am sending you there," he said. "The other is for you two, but it is not to be opened until you are safely settled in Valley Forge." He took the cocked hat which Gil held out to him and threw his traveling cloak over his arm. "I'll write to you just as soon as I can find someone who will carry a letter," he promised. "Take care of each other till I get back."

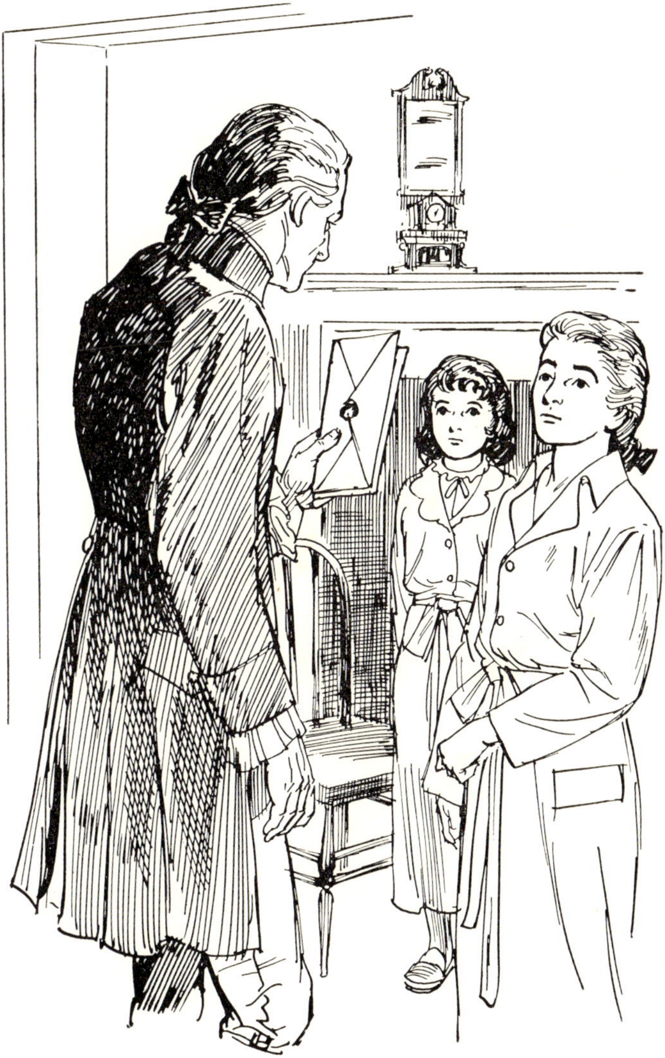

Silver for General Washington

Catching Jenifer to him in a great hug, he planted a kiss on the top of her head, then shook hands solemnly with Gil. A moment later he was running down the white stone steps to the street. By the light of Ezra's lantern Jenifer and her brother saw him mount his horse and wave good-by as he rode off into the night. They listened until they could no longer hear the clatter of his horse's hoofs. Then, feeling a little lost and rather forlorn, they turned and went into the house.

Martha met them in the hall, wiping her eyes on the corner of her apron.

"You jes' hurry back to your beds now, both of you," she commanded. "I want you to git a little snatch of sleep before you has to leave." And thrusting a candle into Gil's hand she shooed them upstairs.

Tumbling into his bed, Gil fell asleep almost at once. But for a long time Jenifer lay awake, staring into the darkness, wondering where her father had gone and what would happen to Gil and herself at Valley Forge. At last she, too, snuggled down into the pillows, closed her eyes, and slept.

CHAPTER TWO

Gil Loses a Letter

O**N EITHER** side of the highway leading from Philadelphia to the west, tall goldenrod and asters drooped under the heat of the blazing sun. Dust lay thick on the leaves and grasses and drifted in clouds through the open windows of the Emmets' family coach, covering everything inside with a film of gray.

Impatiently Gil bent over and blew it from the top of the violin case which lay across his knees. Then he sighed. He was as hungry as a bear in spite of the huge pile of hot cakes and honey which Martha had set before him at breakfast. He was tired of riding, too, for he had been on the road since daylight. And he had no one to talk with, for Jenifer had fallen asleep in the opposite seat of the carriage.

Silver for General Washington

A horsefly was buzzing around near her nose. Gil reached over and waved the fly away. Then, laying his violin down on the seat beside him, he leaned as far out of the coach window as he dared.

"Hey, Ezra, please stop the horses and let me get up there with you," he shouted.

Ezra looked down at him from the driver's seat.

"It's powerful warm up here, Master Gil," he drawled. "Like to melt you to nothin' at all."

"I don't care, I'm coming anyway," Gilbert declared, and turned the handle of the carriage door.

Obligingly Ezra pulled to one side of the highway and waited while Gil climbed to the high seat beside him. Then he flicked the reins and the faded yellow coach rumbled slowly on its way. It lurched as Ezra guided the horses around a bend in the road. Gil clung to the seat and the coachman muttered under his breath.

"This old rattletrap am goin' to fall to pieces one of these days," he grumbled. "I done tole your pappy again and again that we need a new one, but he jes' say we ain't goin' to git nuthin' new till after the war. Martha, she say she thinks your pappy is sendin' all his money and everythin' else he

Gil Loses a Letter

kin git hold of to that there General Washington who is fightin' the redcoats."

He wrinkled his forehead. "Why for does he do that, Master Gil?" he asked. "Why for is all them soldiers fightin'?"

Gil shrugged his shoulders. "I don't know," he said, wiping away the perspiration which trickled down his cheek. "Phew, it's hot, Ezra. How much farther do we have to go?"

"Might be one mile, might be two," Ezra drawled. "Ah ain't been to your Uncle Benjamin's for so long Ah forgits."

"I haven't been there for a long time, either—not since I was a little boy and Jen was a baby," Gil said, and he looked curiously about the country where he and his sister were to spend the next few months.

It was a land of thrifty farmers and prosperous farms. Golden wheat and tasseled corn nodded in the noonday sun. Fat cattle drowsed in the meadows wherever they could find shade. Here and there, close to prim houses of fieldstone or brick, grew well-kept gardens where marigolds, hollyhocks, chrysanthemums, and cosmos bloomed.

Silver for General Washington

Over all the countryside there lay a quiet air of peace and plenty.

Suddenly through the trees Gil caught a glimpse of sunlit water. Then Ezra pointed ahead with his whip to a fieldstone house which stood near the dusty highway, its back to the Schuylkill River.

"There's where you all is goin'," he announced, and pulled his horses up in front of the neat white doorway.

At once Gilbert climbed down over the wheel, intending to arouse Jenifer. But she was already

Gil Loses a Letter

awake and reached the ground as soon as he did. She smiled at her brother as he took his violin from the coach.

"There's a big smudge on your nose, Gilbert Emmet," she said, shaking out her wide skirt and straightening her bonnet. "Your face is all streaky, too."

Without a word Gil wiped his face and brushed the dust from his brown broadcloth breeches. He was feeling a little uncomfortable at the thought of meeting an aunt, uncle, and cousins whom he scarcely knew, but squaring his shoulders he led the way up the path and lifted the heavy brass knocker on the front door.

At first there was no answer although he and Jen could hear the sound reverberating through the house.

"Maybe no one is here and we can go home with Ezra," whispered Jenifer hopefully, for at that moment she wanted more than anything else in the world to be back once more in the quiet, cool house on Chestnut Street. Hardly had she spoken, however, when the door was pulled open by a plump little woman with soft brown hair tucked under a frilled white mobcap, and a big apron almost covering her blue homespun dress. Blinking in the bright sunlight the woman peered first at Jen and then at her brother.

"Why, bless my soul, you're sister Jenifer's children!" she exclaimed at last, putting out her hands to each of them. "Gilbert and little Jen. I'd have known you anywhere even though I've not seen you since you were babies. But where is your father?"

"He couldn't come," Gilbert replied, "but he sent you this." Fishing in the pocket of his coat he pulled from it one of the letters his father had given him, and handed it to his aunt.

Mrs. Gardener broke the seal and unfolded the single sheet of paper. She had almost finished reading what was written there when suddenly a tall, red-haired man with the bluest eyes Gil and Jenifer had ever seen loomed up in the doorway behind her.

"What's all this, Abigail? What's all this?" the big man cried. And he slipped his hands under Mrs. Gardner's elbows and lifted her out of the way as

Gil Loses a Letter

though she were a child. Taking her place on the doorsill he scowled down at Gil.

"Now then, my lad, who are you? Where did you come from? And what in thunderation do you want?"

Dismayed by this greeting, Gil shifted his violin uneasily from one hand to the other and opened his mouth to reply. But Aunt Abigail saved him that trouble.

"These are sister Jenifer's children, Benjamin," she explained quietly, peering around her husband's arm. "They have come to stay with us for a while."

"Good! Good!" boomed Uncle Benjamin. "Get them into the kitchen then so that we can have some dinner before I starve to death. I'll go and help old what's-his-name out there bring in their trunk."

So saying, he strode off down the path to the carriage, where Ezra was busy unfastening the straps which held the leather trunk in place on the rack at the back of the coach.

Aunt Abigail smiled after him affectionately. "Mr. Gardner is always cross when he is hungry,"

Silver for General Washington

she said. "You'll soon learn, just as we have, that it doesn't mean a thing." And she led the bewildered children into the house, down the cool, dark hall to the kitchen.

Here, in spite of the August heat, several logs burned brightly in the great fireplace. Delicious odors of cooking food rose in a steamy cloud from a big pot which swung from the black iron crane over the blaze. On his heels in front of the fire squatted a small boy with hair as red as Uncle Benjamin's, turning a spit which held a large well-browned roast of beef. He stood up when Gilbert and Jenifer entered the room, wiped away the perspiration which was streaming down his face, and came over to his mother.

"This is our Evan," Aunt Abigail said, brushing the child's damp hair back from his forehead. "He is only five but he is such a help to all of us that we could not get along without him." She spoke to the little boy. "Patsy is in the milk shed, molding butter, and Danny is out in the barn," she told him. "Please tell them that your cousins are here from Philadelphia and that dinner is almost ready."

Gil Loses a Letter

Evan, who had been staring curiously at Gilbert and Jenifer, nodded quickly and ran from the room. By the time Jen had laid aside her bonnet and Gilbert had put his fiddle on a cupboard shelf he was back. Sandy-haired Danny, lanky and tall for his thirteen years, and eight-year-old Patsy, who was as chubby and round as her mother, were with him. And before long Gilbert and Jen found themselves seated with the Gardner family at a long table set between two open windows, devouring roast beef with gravy, cold fried chicken, turnips, onions, and greens.

At first there was not much talking, for everyone was hungry and both Gilbert and Jen felt a little embarrassed. But by the time the main part of the meal was finished and Aunt Abigail had helped everyone to a large slice of fresh apple pie, their shyness had vanished. Gil soon found himself describing the events of the previous night, with Jen putting in all the little bits he had forgotten.

"Does your father really believe, then, that the British will attack Philadelphia?" asked Uncle Benjamin rather anxiously.

Silver for General Washington

"Yes, sir," Gil replied, setting down a mug full of milk. "He thinks that the redcoats will march on the city within the next few days."

Aunt Abigail sighed. "Dearie me, we have a lot to be thankful for!" she exclaimed, reaching over to straighten Evan's bib. "Of course, some of the young men from Valley Forge have enlisted in the army. But except for that and for the fact that they are casting guns and making cannon balls over at Colonel Dewees' powder mills and forge we would hardly know that there was a war."

"And there is no reason why we should know it," Uncle Benjamin declared. "Even if the redcoats take the capital they will never come so far inland."

Danny, who was reaching for a piece of gingerbread, stopped with his hand in mid-air. "I wish they would come," he blurted out. "I'd just like to get a shot at one of them."

His father frowned. "You are speaking foolishly and unwisely, Danny," he said severely. "I hold with our Quaker neighbors down the road that all war is wrong. Neither you nor I, my son, are going to have any part in this one."

Gil Loses a Letter

Danny's face flushed and he started to reply. Then, seeing a troubled expression in his mother's eyes, he closed his mouth abruptly. Quickly Aunt Abigail changed the subject and there was no more talk of war during the rest of the meal.

Dinner was over and Jenifer was helping Aunt Abigail and Patsy with the dishes when Ezra, who had eaten his meal in the kitchen shed, appeared in the doorway, hat in hand. He announced that he wanted to start back to Philadelphia at once.

"I let them horses go pretty easy comin' here," he said. "If they gits tired along the way I'll rest them then, but I aches to git back to help Martha close that house and git over to where Sukey lives."

He looked soberly at Gilbert. "Take good care of your sister, Master Gilbert, and you be a good girl, Missy Jen, so that Martha will be proud of the way she's brung you up," he said, and, turning, he started down the steps and around the house.

Gil and Jen and the Gardner children followed him and watched him climb into his high seat and drive away. As the old yellow coach disappeared around the bend in the road, Jen felt a lump rise in her throat, but she swallowed hard. And when

Aunt Abigail suggested a few moments later that she begin unpacking, no one would have suspected that she was feeling homesick already.

It did not take long to remove from the round-topped trunk the things which Martha had laid in it so carefully the night before. Patsy helped Jenifer carry Gil's ruffled shirts, breeches, jackets, long stockings, and shoes to the attic room which he was to share with Evan and Danny. Then she made space in her own closet and bureau drawers for Jen's clothing.

Her blue eyes danced when Jenifer took out her best gown of flowered satin and said rather proudly, "This is my dancing school dress." And she gasped in amazement when she saw the books which lay in the bottom of the Emmets' trunk.

"I never saw so many books in all my life! Can you read all of them?" she asked as Jen set *Robinson Crusoe, Pilgrim's Progress, Gulliver's Travels,* Dillworth's *Speller,* Cocker's *Arithmetick,* and a copy of Foxe's *Book of Martyrs* on the floor.

Jen shook her head. "Not very well," she admitted. "They belong to Gil. I don't like lessons, but I'm learning to read and write and cipher. Fa-

Gil Loses a Letter

ther says I must even if I am a girl, and he has been teaching me himself." She sank back on her heels beside the trunk. "I hope there is a school here in Valley Forge where girls can go as well as boys," she said. "Is there?"

Patsy nodded. "Danny and I both go whenever there is a teacher in the Valley," she said. "Mother has decided that Evan must start, too, this year. I'll show you the school some day soon. It's not far away."

So the two girls talked together, planning all the things they would do during Jenifer's stay in Valley Forge, and by the time the trunk was empty and everything had been put away they were good friends.

Meanwhile Gilbert had gone to the fields to help Danny and his father stack the hay which had been cut that morning. The afternoon passed quickly and there was just time for them to take a swim in the cool waters of the Schuylkill before Uncle Benjamin sent the boys after the cow and her calf which were pastured in a nearby meadow. Then supper was ready. It was not until later that the Emmet children were alone for a few minutes. As they rested on the grass under the apple tree, Jen asked her brother the question which had been in her mind all day.

"Gil, what do you suppose was in the letter Father wrote to us?" she asked. "We're all safely settled now just as he wished. Let's open it."

"All right," agreed Gil. "It's in the pocket of my traveling jacket which I hung on a hook in the attic right after dinner. I'll fetch it." Scrambling to his feet he ran off toward the house.

He was gone so long that Jen began to wonder what had become of him. When at last he returned he looked very unhappy.

"The letter isn't there, Jen," he said miserably. "I've searched in both my jacket pockets and it isn't in either of them."

"Perhaps you dropped it somewhere," Jen suggested. "I'll come and help you look for it."

Carefully she and Gil searched in every place that Gil had been while he was still wearing his traveling jacket. But even though Aunt Abigail, Patsy, and Evan looked too, their hunt was unsuccessful. The letter which Mr. Emmet had written to his children had completely disappeared.

CHAPTER THREE

Things Begin to Happen

AT FIRST Gil was greatly worried over the loss of his father's letter. Jen tried to comfort him.

"What's gone is gone," she said sensibly, and promptly put the whole matter out of her head.

Soon Gil, too, had almost forgotten that the letter had ever existed. This was not difficult. Neither he nor Jenifer had ever lived on a farm before and they found so many new things to do and learn in Valley Forge that they were busy from morning until night.

Before the first week was over Gil was helping Danny with all his chores. Together the boys fed the chickens, geese, and pigs, brought in the wood for the fireplace, filled the water pails, gathered fruit, milked the cows, and worked in the fields whenever they were needed. Yet they still found time to swim in the Schuylkill River or to fish in Trout Run; to play stool-ball, prisoner's base, or leapfrog with the boys of the village; or to visit the forge at Valley Creek.

Gil thought that this forge, where men were making guns and cannon balls for General Washington's army, was the most exciting place in Valley Forge. Despite the fact that it was two miles or more from the Gardners' house, he went there again and again. Often he ventured so close to the gunsmiths that they had to warn him away, lest they shower him with flying sparks when they hammered the white-hot metal into shape on their anvils, or scald him with hissing steam when they plunged the metal into water to cool it.

He never tired of watching the ironworkers as they dipped their ladles into kettles full of gleaming molten metal and then poured the fiery stuff carefully into the molds which shaped the cannon balls. And he felt a thrill of pride each time he saw the completed balls laid out in rows to cool before they were stored away.

Once, when Danny was too busy to go to the forge with him, Gil took Jen over to see it, but she did not like the heat and the noise and the dirt. Also she had many other things to do.

When Aunt Abigail and Patsy made applesauce to be stored in a big barrel in the cellar for winter use, Jen pared and cut apples until her fingers ached. She gathered late berries to be made into pies. She helped Aunt Abigail with her Saturday baking, sniffing with delight at the fragrant bread and cakes when they were lifted on the long-handled peel from the brick oven behind the fireplace. She took her turn at churning butter. She learned how to set up a stocking on Patsy's knitting needles.

Sometimes when the household tasks were finished she and Patsy wandered into the woods to gather wild flowers or to search for oak and sassafras bark, which made splendid yellow, brown, and orange dyes. And often they visited with Patsy's friends, Priscilla Stephens and Betty Walker, who lived nearby. By the time school opened both Jenifer and Gilbert knew so many of the boys and girls of the village that they felt quite at home.

At first Gil, who had been attending the Academy in Philadelphia, did not think much of the tiny one-room schoolhouse with its rows of hard wooden benches and its dunce's stool in the corner. He didn't think much of the teacher, either.

The schoolmaster's long brown coat was covered with spots. His silver buttons were tarnished. His white, ruffled shirt needed washing. His breeches were patched. And his wig was always slightly awry. Gil soon learned, however, that in spite of his untidy dress, Mr. Haskell was a firm

Things Begin to Happen

and kindly gentleman who demanded the very best work possible from every one of his fifteen pupils.

As for Jenifer, she liked both the teacher and the school at first sight. And she found that studying her lessons aloud with the rest of the class was much more fun than doing them alone, as she had in Philadelphia.

The days passed pleasantly and peacefully. Once a party of scouts from the American army rode through the village, bringing news that the British had landed at last in Maryland in a little place called Elkton, and that Washington's soldiers were marching to meet them. But there was as a rule not much talk of war in Valley Forge. Except for the fact that Jenifer and Gilbert missed their father and wondered where he was and what he was doing, they were very happy.

One day, however, something happened which was to cause a change in their lives and in the lives of everyone else in the little village.

It was on a cool brisk evening in mid-September. The whole family had gathered before the big fire in the kitchen. Aunt Abigail and the girls were

Silver for General Washington

knitting; Danny was whittling a cheese-ladder for his mother; and Evan was sprawled on the floor playing with a new kitten which one of the neighbors had given him. Uncle Benjamin had brought out his flute. Gil had his violin, on which he practiced faithfully every day, and the two were trying some tunes together when they were interrupted by a pounding on the door. Danny sprang to his feet and went to find out who was there.

He gasped when he opened the door. By the light of the moon he saw a long line of covered wagons standing in the road before the house. On the doorstep was a soldier in a tattered shirt, mud-stained breeches, and a soiled cocked hat.

"Say, bub, can you tell me which way it is to Colonel Dewees' forge?" the soldier asked in a tired voice.

Danny nodded. "Just go out this road till you get to the creek and then follow it south," he said. "It isn't far."

"I'm glad of that," the soldier declared. "I kind of figgered we'd come the wrong way and the horses are nigh tuckered out."

"Where are you all going, driver?" inquired

Uncle Benjamin, who with the rest of the family had stepped up behind Danny.

"We've got some military supplies here we're goin' to store over to the forge. The army has gone on to—" The soldier stopped abruptly. "Say, mister, are you on our side?" he drawled, studying Uncle Benjamin with a keen eye. "Or are you one

Silver for General Washington

of them sneakin' Tories they say lives hereabouts, that sides with the redcoats?"

Uncle Benjamin's face reddened. "I'm not taking sides with anybody," he declared angrily. "I'm just an honest farmer trying to do my work in peace."

"There ain't much chance of that, mister, when your country is fightin'," scoffed the soldier. "Well, it don't matter how you feel, you'll hear the news somewheres, so I might as well be the one to tell you. We marched ourselves off to meet the British and got ourselves licked good and proper in a battle on Brandywine Creek the other day. Lost a lot of men and ten good cannon. But we'll get back at them redcoats and chase 'em clear out of the country before we're done. See if we don't."

He turned on his heel and went down the path. Gil, who was standing beside his uncle, called after him excitedly.

"Is the whole army coming here?" he asked.

"No, sonny, just us who are drivin' the supply wagons," the soldier replied. Picking up a long whip which lay on the wagon seat, he curled it over the head of the lead horse.

Things Begin to Happen

"Get up!" he cried.

Down the line the other drivers echoed his cry. "Get up!" Horses strained at their traces, wheels creaked, and the heavy wagons loaded with barrels of flour and horseshoes, axes, shovels, and other tools needed for building entrenchments began to move on slowly in the direction of the storehouses near Colonel Dewees' forge.

For some time the Gardners, with Gilbert and Jen, stood on the step watching the great wagons rumble by in the moonlight. Then Aunt Abigail called the whole family inside and shut the door.

"I don't like this!" she exclaimed, leading the way back to the kitchen. "It brings the war too close to home." She looked at her husband. "You know, Benjamin, I have a feeling in my bones that trouble is coming into Valley Forge right in the tracks of those wagon wheels."

"Fiddle-faddle!" Uncle Benjamin snorted, poking up the fire. "You worry like an old mother hen over nothing at all, Abby."

Nevertheless, not many days had passed before Uncle Benjamin was forced to admit that Aunt Abigail had been right.

CHAPTER FOUR

The Enemy Arrives

IT WAS on a cloudy afternoon several days after the arrival of the supply wagons from General Washington's army that the trouble which Aunt Abigail had predicted came to Valley Forge. As luck would have it, Uncle Benjamin had driven a wagonload of vegetables to the market in Germantown, expecting to be gone for two days. Aunt Abigail, too, was away. Having been called that very morning to nurse a sick aunt in Swedesford, a short way down the river, she had ridden off with Uncle Benjamin, taking Evan with her. The other four children were in school.

Gilbert and Danny sat on a wooden bench figuring sums in big brown paper copybooks. Over on the girls' side of the room Jenifer was studying

The Enemy Arrives

her spelling aloud, and Patsy was copying her writing lesson with a goose-quill pen which Mr. Haskell had just cut for her. Suddenly the door to the schoolhouse was thrust open. Sam Jones, one of the apprentices at the forge, burst into the room.

"The British are coming, Mr. Haskell!" Sam panted. "The British are coming!"

The schoolmaster dropped his book. "How do you know?" he asked sharply.

"Jim Bates saw them out past Perkiomen Creek and galloped in to give warning," Sam replied excitedly. "Colonel Dewees is trying to get the army supplies moved across the river before they get here, but he needs a lot of men to help him. Can you go, Mr. Haskell?"

"At once!" replied Mr. Haskell promptly.

"Hurry!" Sam shot out of the door and dashed off to spread his disturbing news and to get more aid in moving the precious tools, weapons, and supplies out of reach of the advancing enemy.

For almost a minute there was complete silence in the schoolroom. The children stared blankly at one another, not knowing what to say or do. Then several of the boys began to talk at once and two of

Silver for General Washington

the smaller girls started to cry. Mr. Haskell rapped on his desk for order. His eyes scanned the room quickly and he spoke the names of the four biggest boys.

"Stephen, John, Thomas, Daniel, if you want to help at the forge, come along. The rest of you get your things and go to your homes at once. Tell your parents that the British are coming to the village. If God and the redcoats permit, I will open school tomorrow as usual and will expect to find you all in your seats. Now go, and the good Lord watch over you."

He stepped quietly to the back of the room and held the door open while the boys and girls gathered their things together hurriedly and set out for their homes. Gilbert, Jenifer, and Patsy were the last to leave. As they started up the road they saw the schoolmaster with Danny and the other boys go racing across the meadow and through the woods in the direction of the forge.

Gil looked after them enviously, wishing that he, too, had been chosen to help save the army supplies. Then he walked slowly away from the schoolhouse, holding his head high in the air, just

The Enemy Arrives

to show that he wasn't afraid of the redcoats or anything they might do. But Jen and Patsy were running and soon Gil found himself running too.

The way home was long. When the three children reached the safety of the house at last they were so out of breath that they could not speak, but stood in the middle of the kitchen floor looking at one another. All at once Patsy began to cry.

"I want my mother," she sobbed. "I don't want the old British to come. I want my mother."

Hastily Jenifer slipped a comforting arm around her. "Don't, Patsy, you mustn't cry," she said. She turned to her brother. "What are we going to do, Gil?" she asked.

"Yes," Patsy choked in a miserable voice, "what are we going to do?"

Gil's heart sank. For the first time he realized that, with Danny away, he was the oldest and must take charge of the situation. He knew, too, that no matter what happened he must never let the girls know that he was really as frightened as they were. So he tried to make his voice sound as calm as possible when he spoke.

"The first thing to do, I guess, is to remember

Silver for General Washington

that even though the redcoats are our enemies they are people just like us," he declared. "They aren't coming here to hurt us. They are just coming to capture General Washington's supplies."

"Maybe we won't even see them, then!" Patsy exclaimed, sniffling hopefully.

"Maybe not," Gil agreed. "But in case they should come here I think we'd better hide the things we don't want them to take away, just as Father and I did in Philadelphia. What are the most valuable things in the house?"

"That silver dish!" Patsy said, pointing to a plate on the top shelf of the cupboard. "And the spoons that Grandma gave Mother on her wedding day, and the box Father keeps his hard money in, and his gun, and—and the chickens! I don't want them to take the chickens, Gil."

Gilbert scratched his head. "I don't either," he agreed. "Ezra told me once that soldiers always took chickens if they could find them. But chickens are hard to hide."

"Put them in the cellar," Jenifer suggested. "It's dark there and maybe they won't make a noise. We must leave a few in the henhouse, though, so

The Enemy Arrives

that the British won't suspect that we have hidden some and begin to look for them."

Gil nodded. "We better begin right away," he said.

Quickly Jenifer picked up the silver dish, gathered the spoons together, and ran upstairs to tuck them all under the covers of Evan's trundle bed. Patsy took her father's money box from the corner cupboard and hid it in the oven behind the fireplace. And Gil carried the gun out to the woodshed and stuck it under some logs. Then all three children went to the chicken yard.

Catching chickens, they soon found, was no easy task. The bewildered birds squawked and cackled and fluttered their wings until the air was filled with flying feathers. At the end of an hour only eleven of the twenty birds were safe in the cellar.

"We'd better leave the others where they are," Gil said, sucking a place on his hand where one of the frightened fowls had pecked him. He carried a pan of water downstairs while Patsy and Jenifer scattered some grain on the dirt floor. Then Gil shut the cellar door and he and the girls hurried back to the kitchen.

It was growing dark and the house, which always seemed empty when Aunt Abigail and Uncle Benjamin were away, now seemed more forlorn than ever. In the excitement of moving the chickens the three children had almost forgotten about the redcoats. Now they all remembered at once, and each one tried to hide from the other the fact that he was afraid.

Glancing at the tall clock in the corner Jenifer saw that it was after six.

"Aunt Abigail told me that if she wasn't home by this time it meant that she had had to spend the night in Swedesford and that I must get supper," she said. And she set about heating the corn-meal

The Enemy Arrives

mush which her aunt had left ready for the evening meal. Gil brought in another log for the fire and lighted the candles, while Patsy began to set the table. Just as she lifted four porringers from the cupboard shelf the kitchen door opened and Danny came in. He had been running and was out of breath. But Jenifer, Patsy, and Gil began to ply him with questions at once.

"Danny, are you all right?"

"Did the British come?"

"Could you save the supplies?"

"Where are the redcoats, Danny? Will the redcoats come to our house?"

"I don't know," said Danny in reply to this last question from Patsy. "They went into Colonel Dewees' house and stole everything they could lay their hands on and smashed the furniture and ripped the curtains to pieces. And they captured all the supplies before we could save any of them and set fire to the storehouses and the forge."

"Set fire to the forge!" Gil exclaimed in dismay.

Danny nodded soberly. "It had burned almost to the ground when I left," he declared. "There are hundreds of redcoats here in the village, Gil, mak-

Silver for General Washington

ing camp along the river up past Fatland Ford. The Hessians are with them, too."

"What are Hessians?" Patsy asked fearfully, moving closer to her brother.

"German soldiers," Danny explained. "The British have hired them to help fight us. The Hessians are the ones who did all the damage in Colonel Dewees' house. They stole five geese from old Peter Means, too, and killed one of his pigs and——"

Jenifer interrupted him. "We hid some chickens in the cellar."

"Good!" exclaimed Danny. "We ought to hide Bessie and her calf, too. I know a place in the woods where they'll be safe. We can milk Bess after we drive them there. Come on, Gil."

He ran to the milk shed, grabbed a pail, and set off for the meadow where the cow and calf were pastured, with Gil close at his heels.

It seemed to Patsy and Jen that the two boys were gone for hours. Jen was sure that there had never before been so many strange noises about the house, and once Patsy thought she saw a face at the window. But nothing happened, no one

The Enemy Arrives

came, and the boys returned at last with a pail full of milk. They reported that they had not met any redcoats or Hessians on the road.

"They must be camping over near the forge," Danny said. He looked at the table, on which Patsy and Jenifer had set bread, butter, honey, a plate of doughnuts, and a big pitcher of milk. "Isn't supper ready yet?" he asked. "I'm hungry enough to eat cannon balls."

"All ready," Jen declared. And she dished out the steaming corn-meal mush.

Everyone sat down and bowed his head, while Danny, who had taken his father's seat at the table, asked the blessing.

"We thank Thee, O Lord, for the food which——" Danny began. But he got no further. At that very moment there was a heavy tramping of feet on the back steps. The kitchen door was pushed open suddenly. And three brass-capped, green-coated soldiers, each with a long, drooping mustache, appeared on the threshold.

"They're Hessians!" Danny exclaimed under his breath, and he jumped up so quickly that his chair fell over backwards with a clatter.

CHAPTER FIVE

Unwelcome Visitors

For one long, terrifying moment the three Hessian soldiers stood in the doorway looking all about the candle-lit kitchen. Then Danny stepped up to them bravely.

"This is our house," he declared loudly, blurting out the first words which came into his mind. "This is our house and you can't come into it."

Muttering something to his companions which Danny could not understand, the foremost Hessian grabbed the boy by the shoulder.

"Man—fadder—iss here?" he asked, saying the words slowly.

Wishing with all his heart that his father could walk into the room at that very instant, Danny shook his head.

"Goot!" exclaimed the Hessian. Pushing the boy aside he strode into the kitchen, followed by

Unwelcome Visitors

the two other soldiers. They crossed the room to the table, which Gil and the girls had left hastily, and surveyed the uneaten meal. Picking up a loaf of bread, one of them tore off a hunk with his teeth. Another growled something in German, and the man who had spoken to Danny turned to the children who stood together in a frightened group near the fireplace.

"Meat we will haf!" he demanded roughly. "Meat und beer."

Danny nodded. "Give them plenty to eat and then perhaps they won't take anything else," he told Gil and the girls, speaking softly because he was afraid that one of the other soldiers might be able to understand English. "Is there any meat in the closet?"

"There's half a ham," Jenifer whispered, trying to stiffen her knees so that they wouldn't knock together.

"Good!" exclaimed Danny. "You fetch that and Gil and I will get some beer from the cellar."

"Don't forget that the chickens are down there," Jen warned him under her breath. "Don't wake them up."

Silver for General Washington

Danny shook his head. He took a jug from the cupboard shelf, Gil picked up a candle, and the two boys started for the cellar. By the time they were back with the beer Patsy had gathered together enough courage to put two more loaves of her mother's good bread on the table. And Jenifer had set the ham and some plates before the soldiers, clattering the dishes together as noisily as possible to cover up any cackling the chickens might make if they were aroused.

The Hessians ate ravenously, washing down meat and bread with great gulps of beer. They glanced about uneasily as they devoured their food, and said little to one another. At last one of them decided that he had had enough. He wiped his drooping mustache on the corner of the table cover, stood up, and began to walk about the room, examining the furniture curiously, pulling open the closet door and peering into the cupboard.

Gil's violin lay on the table near the door, for he had been practicing duets with Uncle Benjamin the night before and had neglected to put it away. All at once the Hessian soldier spied it.

"Ach! Musik!" he exclaimed. Picking up the

fiddle he drew the bow across the strings once or twice and began to play a lively tune. But his companions had finished eating. Stuffing what remained of the ham and bread in their pockets they pushed back their chairs.

"Kommst du, Hans. Komm'," one of them cried and started for the door.

Still playing, Hans followed them.

From the moment the Hessian had first laid

Silver for General Washington

hands on his violin, Gil had been watching him anxiously, fearful that he might hurt the instrument in some way. Now suddenly he realized that the man intended to walk off with it.

"Hey!" he cried, running to the soldier and catching at his jacket. "That's my violin."

The Hessian turned quickly. Holding the fiddle high out of Gil's reach, he laughed down at the boy. "Mine violin," he taunted. "Mine."

"No, no," shouted Gil angrily. "Give it to me!" And quite beside himself at the thought of losing his precious fiddle he yanked at the man's arm with all his strength.

With a snarl of rage the Hessian slapped the boy so hard on the side of his head that he fell in a heap on the floor. Then, tucking the violin under his jacket, the soldier dashed out of the door. Danny, who had sprung to Gil's assistance, saw all three Hessians disappear down the road.

Although his head was throbbing, Gil insisted stoutly that he was not really hurt when Danny and Jenifer helped him to his feet.

"But my violin is gone," he said forlornly, as he sat down before the fire with his elbows on his

Unwelcome Visitors

knees. "It's gone, and I'll never have another one." And he looked so unhappy that no one had the heart to rejoice outwardly over the fact that the soldiers had taken nothing else and that the eleven chickens were still safely hidden in the cellar.

Jenifer, Patsy, and Danny cleared up the mess which the Hessians had made of the supper table. Then Jen suggested that as long as the soldiers hadn't eaten the corn-meal mush, she might as well heat it up again.

"We'll all feel better if we have something to eat," she said sensibly.

So she warmed the mush and, because Patsy refused to sit down so soon at a table where the hateful Hessians had been, the four children ate their supper sitting close to the fire, with their porringers in their laps.

"Let's all sleep right here in the kitchen tonight," Patsy suggested as she began to gather up the empty porringers. "We can keep the candles burning all night and I won't be half so scared as if I were in a room alone with Jen."

This seemed a good plan, and beds were quickly made up on the floor, since everyone except Danny

Silver for General Washington

was tired. Danny brought his father's gun from the woodshed where Gil had hidden it and announced that he would stand guard all night in case the Hessians should return.

"Gil ought to go to bed because of his headache," he said, "but I'm so wide awake that I feel as though I would never go to sleep again."

Nevertheless, it was not long after the others were slumbering soundly that Danny's head began to nod. Soon he, too, was fast asleep with the gun across his knees. The candles melted and flickered out. The fire burned low. No one disturbed the sleeping children and the tall clock in the corner slowly ticked the hours away. Morning came at last—a clear crisp autumn morning.

Gil was the first to awaken. For a moment he lay still in his bed on the floor, wondering where he was, and why his head hurt, and what had happened to make him feel so heavyhearted. Then he remembered about the visit of the Hessians and the loss of his violin. A faint hope came to him that perhaps the soldier had changed his mind about taking away the fiddle and left it on the doorstep or hidden in the bushes nearby. Pushing back the

Unwelcome Visitors

quilt which Jenifer had laid over him, he scrambled to his feet and went outside to look. Before long he came hurrying back.

"Danny, Danny," he cried excitedly, shaking his cousin by the shoulder, "there's not a single chicken left in the chicken yard and one of the pigs is gone."

Danny opened his eyes and blinked sleepily. Patsy and Jenifer also awoke and all three stared unbelievingly at Gil.

"I didn't hear a sound out there," Danny said at last, fingering his father's gun and looking a little uncomfortable. "The Hessians must have come back and stolen the chickens after I fell asleep."

Jenifer stood up and shook out her skirts. "What about the ones we put in the cellar, Gil?" she asked.

"They are all right," Gil declared. "I went down to see. The stupid things think that it is still night and they're sound asleep."

This was good news. Gil and the girls felt rather proud of themselves that they had succeeded in saving some of the fowls, and Patsy wanted to bring them out of the cellar at once because she thought that they would be happier in the daylight. But

Silver for General Washington

Danny said the hens had better stay where they were until he was sure that there were no more Hessians about. Also he was worried about Bessie.

" If Bessie isn't milked she'll start bellowing and then someone is bound to find both of them," he said. "I'll attend to her and do a little exploring, too." And taking his pail he set out at once.

He was gone for some time. When he returned he was empty-handed.

"There are so many redcoats around that I didn't even try to bring the milk back for fear they would ask me where it came from and then take Bessie away from us," he explained. "I just poured it out on the ground and hid the pail in some bushes. Then I walked down the road as far as Doctor Stephens' house. There are soldiers camping all along both sides of the river and a company of Hessians have pitched their tents right where we went swimming this summer."

"Did you see anyone except the soldiers?" Jenifer asked.

Danny nodded. "I met Abner Coles. Three of the British officers have moved right into his house. They are very polite, he says, but they eat like

Unwelcome Visitors

wolves and his mother has to spend all her time cooking for them. Some redcoats stole Abner's black horse last night, too. When I met him he was on his way to ask General Howe to make them give her back."

"General William Howe?" Gil asked eagerly. "Which way was Abner going, Danny? Did he tell you where the General is staying? Can I overtake him if I run fast enough?"

So rapidly did Gil's questions follow one another that Danny couldn't help grinning.

"Why are you in such a hurry?" he asked slowly. "What do you care where General Howe has his headquarters?"

"Oh, don't you see, Danny?" Gil cried impatiently. "It's my violin. If Abner can get his horse back maybe I can get my violin."

Danny whistled. "Maybe you can," he exclaimed. "Listen, Gil. Do you know where William Grimes lives, out past Bull Tavern? Well, that's where General Howe is staying. Abner says——"

But what else Abner had said Gil was never to know, for he was halfway upstairs on the way to

Silver for General Washington

the attic room which he shared with his cousin before Danny had finished his sentence. If he were going to call on a general, Gil thought, he must look as neat as possible. Nevertheless, he knew that he would have no time to change his clothes if he hoped to overtake Abner. So, snatching up his cocked hat and the traveling jacket which he had not worn since his arrival in Valley Forge, he hurried downstairs again. Shouting good-by to Jen and his cousins, he ran out the front door.

Just as he limped hastily down the path a company of redcoats was marching past the house. They paid no attention to him, however, and he was glad that his way led in the opposite direction from the one they were taking. He met no other soldiers, but as he crossed the Fatland Ford road he caught his first glimpse of their camp, which stretched along both banks of the Schuylkill River as far as the eye could see.

At any other time he would have stopped to watch the swarms of red-and-blue-coated men who were cooking their food over campfires, washing out their clothes in the river, cleaning their muskets, and preparing themselves and their weap-

Unwelcome Visitors

ons for their next battle with the Americans. At any other time he would also have noticed the odor of smoldering wood which hung heavy in the air, the blackened barns set afire by the Germans the previous night, and the smoke still rising from the ruins of Colonel Dewees' storehouses and forge.

Now, however, he hurried along, half running, half walking, with only one thought in his mind—to get back his beloved fiddle.

He had passed Bull Tavern before he caught sight of Abner Coles. The older boy was standing in the entrance of William Grimes' house arguing with a sentry. As Gil ran up the path the soldier cried out at Abner in exasperation. "Look here, you young rebel," he shouted. "I've told you three times that you cannot see the General this morning. Now take yourself off before I prick you full of holes with my bayonet."

He lunged threateningly at Abner. Quick as a flash the boy ducked to one side. The soldier lost his balance. With an oath he fell to the ground. By the time he had picked himself up, Abner and Gil had thrust the door open and both were safely inside the house.

CHAPTER SIX

"I'll Find a Way"

THE HALL was dimly lighted and at first Gil and Abner did not see the red-coated officer who stood before them. They were startled when he spoke.

"Whatever do you miserable young ruffians mean by bursting into this house in such an unseemly fashion?" he asked sharply. "Don't you know that the General is making his headquarters here?"

"Yes," Abner blurted out. "That's why——" He broke off suddenly as someone behind him laid a heavy hand on his shoulder and the sentry spoke up.

"These young devils sneaked right past me, Major," the sentry declared, digging his fingers into Abner's flesh. "I didn't want to shoot two young lads, I didn't, and I was just arguing with them when they gave me the slip. But now, sir, I'll

"I'll Find a Way"

take them out and deal with them as they deserves."

"I won't go out," Abner cried angrily, shaking off the sentry's grasp with a quick movement of his shoulder. "I want to see General Howe. Some of his soldiers took my horse last night and I came here to get her back again."

"They stole my violin, too," Gil added breathlessly. "It's the one my father gave me. A Hessian——"

From the room to the right of the hall a deep voice interrupted him.

"What's going on out there, Major Banks? If anyone wants to see me and has managed to get past that confounded sentry, let him come in at once."

"Very well, General Howe," the young officer replied stiffly. To the sentry he said, "Get back to your post." Then, stepping aside, he allowed the boys to pass him and followed them into the room from which the voice had come.

A stout, elderly man, in a scarlet coat heavily trimmed with gold lace and braid, was seated at a long table on which a map was spread. He swung around in his chair and a look of surprise crossed his face when he saw his visitors.

Silver for General Washington

"You needn't wait, Major Banks," he said, with an amused smile. "I think I can deal with our youthful friends without your help."

Saluting smartly, the major left the room.

General Howe leaned back in his chair and folded his hands over his stomach.

"Well, my lads," he said, "I trust I see before me two loyal subjects of the King. You must have very pressing errands or you would not have pushed your way in past the sentry." He looked at Gil. "Suppose you speak up first and tell me what brought you here."

"Yes, sir," Gil said. His heart was beating furiously, now that he was actually standing before the great General Howe, and it seemed to him that his tongue was suddenly glued to the roof of his mouth. But he stammered out a sentence or two and soon the words were spilling from his lips, as he told the story of the theft of his violin. All the time he was talking General Howe watched him closely. When he had finished the General did not speak to him, but turned to ask Abner what he had to say. Briefly the older boy explained that his horse had been taken from him.

"I'll Find a Way"

"One of your officers is quartered in our house," Abner said in finishing. "He told me that you had forbidden your soldiers to steal from us. He said that you would punish the men who took my horse and help me get her back."

General Howe stroked his chin thoughtfully. "It is true that my men have been ordered to pay for everything which they take," he said slowly. "Sometimes, unfortunately, they forget this order. I will gladly see that the soldiers who robbed you are punished, make them return your horse, and give back your young friend's violin, providing——" He hesitated a moment. "Providing that you two will do a small service for me."

"What's that?" Gil asked eagerly.

"Look here," General Howe said. He motioned the boys to come closer and pointed to a spot on the map which lay before him. "This is Valley Forge, where we are. Here is the Schuylkill River. Here, not ten miles away, is the village of Trappe. Now, I have been told that General Washington and his army are camping near Trappe. I would like to have you boys cross the river and find the American camp.

"Walk about among the soldiers. Talk to them. Try to discover how many there are, what condition their weapons are in, how long they intend to stay near Trappe, and where they plan to go next. When you have returned and made your report to me, I will see that each of you is given back what has been taken from you." He looked at the boys. "Will you do it?" he asked.

"I'll Find a Way"

For a moment neither boy replied. Then Gil shook his head slowly.

"I couldn't do that even to get my fiddle back again," he declared.

"But surely you could do it to help your King!" General Howe exclaimed.

"I haven't any king," Gil said solemnly.

With an exclamation of annoyance General Howe turned to Abner. Already the older boy had started for the door.

"Here, here, where are you going?" the General asked. "Don't you want your horse?"

Abner swung around. His eyes were blazing. "No, sir, not if I have to spy on our own army to get her," he declared.

"You won't be spying on an army," the General argued. "You will only be finding out for me what mischief an unruly mob of rebels is planning. Why, I am giving you lads an opportunity to be of real service to your King—a service for which you will be well paid. In addition to seeing that you have your horse and your violin again, I will give you each six guineas—good hard golden guineas that will buy a hundred times more than the paper

Silver for General Washington

money which the rebels use. Don't you think that is a generous offer?"

"Generous enough," Abner admitted grudgingly, "but I am not a King's man and I won't do it."

"I won't either," Gil added firmly.

General Howe shrugged his shoulders. "You may change your minds when you have had time to think it over. If you do, come back and let me know. And remember," he said evenly as he drummed with his fingers on the table, "remember that stubborn boys are often sorry boys."

"What did he mean by that last remark?" Gil asked Abner after the two boys had left the house, passed the glowering sentry without a word, and started off toward home.

Abner shrugged his shoulders. "I don't know," he said. "It was a threat of some kind, but I'm not going to let it fret me. There are half a dozen people around here who would do the old man's spying for him, if he only knew it."

"King's people?" Gil asked.

"Uh-huh," agreed Abner. "King's people or Tories or whatever you want to call them. They'll

"I'll Find a Way"

do anything they can to help the redcoats win. But they're not half so bad, to my way of thinking, as those who don't care which side wins as long as they don't have to do anything about it. Well——" He stopped, for they had come to the bridge over Valley Creek. "This is the way I go. Too bad we didn't both have better luck," he said. And he started off in the direction of the ruined forge, leaving Gil to trudge on alone.

It was now midday. The redcoats and Hessians were at their noon meal and few of the villagers were abroad. Except for an old man who sold baskets from door to door, Gil did not see anyone he knew. He was glad, for he did not feel like talking. His lame leg ached. He was sick with disappointment over the failure of his errand. And he was missing his father more than he had ever missed him before.

One talk with his father would, he knew, answer the muddle of questions in his mind. The war against the British had been going on for so long and had, until now, seemed so far away that he had thought little about it. He had not even listened very attentively the few times his father had dis-

Silver for General Washington

cussed it with him. With the coming of the enemy to Valley Forge he had suddenly found himself right in the midst of it and there were a great many things which he wanted to know.

What did it really mean to be a King's man? How had the war started? What was the fighting all about anyway? Where was his father and how was he helping General Washington?

He was thinking so hard about all these things that he did not notice that the sun had disappeared and the rain clouds were piling up in the east. The first drops began to fall as he turned into the path that led to the Gardners' house. Someone had locked the front door in his absence and the kitchen door was shut fast, too. When he knocked, Jenifer opened it a crack, and peered out cautiously before she let him in. She was alone in the kitchen.

"Where are the others?" Gil asked, shaking the raindrops from his cocked hat.

"Aunt Abigail came home just after you left," his sister told him. "She said children had to go to school, war or no war, and she walked over with Danny and Patsy and Evan to see if Mr. Haskell is teaching today. I stayed here to wait for you."

"I'll Find a Way"

She looked at Gil. "Didn't you get your violin?"

"No," her brother replied shortly, and slumping down in a chair with his hands plunged deep into the pockets of his long jacket, he began to tell what had happened during his visit to General Howe. He had almost finished the story when a puzzled expression crossed his face.

"Hey, what's this?" he asked in surprise, as he groped for something that seemed to be in his jacket pocket. "Look, Jen, there's a tear in the lining. Something has slipped through it and is 'way down in this corner of the coat. It feels like paper. Here, help me get it out."

He held the pocket wide open while Jenifer stuck her hand through the rent in the lining. After a moment she pulled out a packet of paper which had been folded twice and sealed with red wax.

"It's—why, it's Father's letter," she cried joyfully, turning it over and over in her hands. "Oh, Gil, I thought we'd never find it, and there it's been all the time. Here, hurry up and read it, please." Thrusting the letter at her brother, Jenifer pulled a chair close to his and waited for him to begin.

With eager fingers Gil broke the seal and unfolded the sheets of paper. At the sight of his father's firm, neat handwriting a warm feeling of comfort stole over him and he felt happier than he had all day.

"It's a good long one," he said with satisfaction. Settling back in his chair he cocked one knee over the other and began reading slowly.

"My dear children,

"When you open this letter you will be settled in Valley Forge—safe, I hope, from all

"I'll Find a Way"

the dangers and discomforts of the war. I shall be on the ocean, bound for a foreign land where I intend, if possible, to get money and other help for our army.

"Because I have always wanted you to be happy and carefree I have seldom discussed the war with you. Now the time has come when you must understand clearly whom we are fighting and why. I have already explained to you how the thirteen American colonies were settled over a hundred years ago by people from Europe. As you know, our colonies were governed for many years by England and paid taxes to her. Sometimes they have disagreed with their mother country but, until recently, they have always loved her and obeyed her.

"Now, however, things are changed. King George the Third, who is ruling England at present, is a stubborn and a stupid man. For years he has been treating his American subjects very badly, making foolish, unjust laws for us, and ordering us to pay taxes which are unnecessary and unfair.

Silver for General Washington

"When Mr. Benjamin Franklin tried to ask him to change these laws and taxes, and to let us help in governing our own country, King George would not even listen. Instead he sent soldiers over here to shoot or arrest everyone who would not obey him. This made us little better than slaves, and forced us to go to war against him.

"At first we fought only to be free of King George and his followers. Now we are fighting for something much greater. We want to be free of all kings. We believe, as our Declaration of Independence states, that 'all men are created equal, that they are endowed by their Creator with certain unalienable rights, that among these are Life, Liberty and the pursuit of Happiness.'

"Independence for our country, and liberty for all men—these things are worth fighting for. And to win them we Americans have pledged 'our Lives, our Fortunes, and our sacred Honor.'

"I expect to return to you safely. But if anything should happen to prevent this, Un-

"I'll Find a Way"

cle Benjamin will attend to my business affairs and take care of you. Meanwhile, if you or he need money for anything important, remember that the silver which will lie buried in the chest down cellar can easily be sold and should fetch a good price. The British may capture Philadelphia, but they will not hold it long, for our army will not cease fighting until it has driven every one of King George's soldiers from our land. If, by any chance, either of you is ever able to help in this fight I know that you will do so bravely and well, no matter how difficult the task may be.

"Obey Aunt Abigail and Uncle Benjamin and take care of each other until I return. I will write to you both again just as soon as it is possible to send a letter. God bless you always and keep you safely.

"Your loving Father."

Gil looked up. "That's all there is," he told his sister, "except the date, August 21, 1777, and two lines down here at the bottom of the page. They say 'Please destroy this letter. It might bring harm

Silver for General Washington

to all of us if it should fall into the hands of the enemy.'"

"What shall we do with it?" Jenifer asked, looking anxiously at her brother.

"Burn it," Gil declared. "But I don't want to. It's almost like having Father in the room with us, to read what he has written. Would you like to hear it once more?"

Jen nodded, so Gil read the letter slowly through again and yet again. Then solemnly he tore the sheets of paper into little bits and laid them on the fire. Together he and Jenifer watched the flames take them and turn them to ashes.

That night, long after the others had fallen asleep, Gil lay with wide-open eyes, thinking about his father's letter.

"Independence for our country!" "Liberty for all men!" These were gallant words and they marched through Gil's mind as brave soldiers march against an enemy. Only one thing disturbed him. How could he, a boy only twelve years old, help his country in her fight for freedom?

"I'll find a way," he promised himself. And then he fell asleep.

CHAPTER SEVEN

Eleven Thousand Hungry Men

FOR TWO days longer the redcoats and the Hessians lingered at Valley Forge. These were days filled with suspense and fear, for no one knew when enemy soldiers might break into his home in search of food, or carry off his cattle and poultry, or steal his grain and flour. When at last the enemy army marched away it was as though a great black cloud had been lifted from the village. At once people began to visit one another to discuss what had happened and to plan how best to help those whose homes and barns had been looted and burned.

When Uncle Benjamin returned from Germantown on the evening of the day that the enemy left, he found several neighbors gathered in his kitchen. Gravely and silently he listened to their stories. His face grew grim as he learned how the Hessians had broken into his own home, stealing

Silver for General Washington

the chickens, the pig, and Gil's violin. But he said little until the neighbors had left and the children were in bed. Then Patsy and Jen, who shared the room over the kitchen, could hear him talking, talking, talking to Aunt Abigail.

Next day, however, things went on about as usual. The chickens were put back in the poultry yard. Bessie and her calf were brought home from the woods. And, before long, the visit of the redcoats and the Hessians to the Gardners' home had come to seem to Danny and the girls like a bad dream. With Gil, though, it was different. Losing his violin was like losing one of his closest friends. When, now and then, Uncle Benjamin took out his flute to play a tune in the evening, Gil longed for his fiddle.

But it was not often that Uncle Benjamin had time to play. With the coming of colder weather there were many things to be done in preparation for winter. This year there were more tasks than ever before, because the people whose property had been stolen or destroyed by the enemy needed so much help.

Everybody worked like a beaver all through Oc-

Eleven Thousand Hungry Men

tober and November. By the time the first snow fell, early in December, shelters had been raised for the cattle, to replace barns which had been burned; damaged houses and furniture had been repaired. Every pumpkin, every ear of corn, every sheaf of wheat had been carefully harvested.

In Aunt Abigail's cellar turnips, onions, cabbages, potatoes, and winter squash, as well as large barrels of apple butter, applesauce, and cider had been safely stored away. Freshly made cheeses were ripening in the springhouse. Fat hams, sausage, bacon, and a side of beef which Uncle Benjamin had bought from a neighboring farmer hung in the smokehouse. Large paper-topped, earthenware crocks filled with jellies, pickles, and preserved fruits stood in neat rows on the shelves of the storeroom. And tucked in the darkest corner of the closet was a whole winter's supply of candles which Jenifer and Patsy had helped to dip.

News had reached the village during the fall that the American army had been defeated again in a battle at Germantown, near Philadelphia, and that the British army had marched into the capital and was planning to spend the winter there. Gil and

Silver for General Washington

Jenifer wondered whether any redcoats or Hessians had broken into their house on Chestnut Street, and hoped that Martha and Ezra had locked it up so securely that no one could get in. Gil thought often of his father's letter. Sometimes at night after he and Danny had gone to bed they talked about the war. Each of them longed for a chance to help the American soldiers.

It was on a Friday, December the nineteenth, that their first chance came. Mr. Haskell, who had been trying to teach school with his jaw all swollen up and tied in his woolen muffler, dismissed his pupils at noon, so that he could go to the blacksmith to have an aching tooth pulled.

Jenifer and Patsy were glad of the unexpected half holiday, for Aunt Abigail was planning a quilting party that afternoon and they wanted to be there to help pass the caraway-seed cookies and Liberty Tea, for which they had gathered the loosestrife leaves. Danny and Gilbert, too, were delighted to have a few free hours so that they could work on the big sled which they were making together. And Evan was pleased, for now he would have some extra time to play with his be-

Eleven Thousand Hungry Men

loved kitten. In great good spirits all five ran off, laughing and shouting along the frozen, rutted road, toward home.

Aunt Abigail was setting up her quilting frame when they burst into the kitchen, blowing on their freezing fingers, stamping their feet, and trying to explain all at once why they were home so early.

"Well, take your things off and put them away," she said, when at last she could make herself heard. "You can eat the lunches that you took to school and I'll give you each a mug of hot milk to warm you up."

She smiled ruefully as she filled a three-legged iron pot with milk and set it close to the fire. "It's a great pity about Mr. Haskell!" she said. "But why did the poor man have to have a toothache today of all days, when I'm expecting——" She lifted her head. "Hark! There's someone knocking on the front door. Go and see who it is, Danny," she said.

Danny tossed his woolen cap to the bench near the fire and left the room. A moment later he returned. Behind him was a stranger—a tall young man whose threadbare greatcoat lacked so many buttons that it gaped open, disclosing a faded

Silver for General Washington

blue army jacket and badly stained buff-colored breeches.

"Lieutenant Moffat of General Varnum's brigade of the American Army at your service, ma'am," the young officer said to Aunt Abigail, lifting his hand in a tired salute.

"Come in, Lieutenant. Come close to the fire and warm yourself," Aunt Abigail said, noticing at once that the man was pale and his lips were blue with cold.

Lieutenant Moffat straightened up and shook his head. "Thank you kindly, but I'm hard pressed for time, ma'am," he said. "Our army is on its way here to Valley Forge to take up winter quarters. They will arrive some time today and my orders are to find suitable quarters for the generals. How many rooms have you in this house?"

"Four, and the attic where the boys sleep," Aunt Abigail replied, slipping her arm around Patsy, who had come to stand beside her.

The lieutenant looked quickly about the kitchen, noting the size of the room and the furnishings. "And how many people are there in your family?"

"Seven, counting my niece and nephew from Philadelphia," replied Aunt Abigail.

"Well, ma'am, I hardly think you'll be bothered with officers tonight, then," the lieutenant said. "We've been told to quarter them in the larger

Silver for General Washington

houses first and I'm sure there are some in the village with more room to spare than you have here. I'll be going on my way now. Good day to you, ma'am."

He turned to go, but Gil, who had been standing impatiently first on one foot and then on the other, blurted out a question.

"Is General Washington coming to Valley Forge, too?" he asked excitedly.

The officer nodded and for the first time he smiled. "He'll be here. He's always where his men are," he said, and swinging on his heel he left the room.

Crowding after him to the door, the children watched him mount the horse which he had tied to the gatepost and ride away. Then they trooped back to the kitchen, where they found Aunt Abigail putting away her quilting frame.

"There'll be no quilting party here today," she told them. "If the rest of the army looks as poorly as that young man, it must be in a bad way. He seemed half-sick and starved to death." She picked up a pail. "Here, Gil, get some water from the spring. Jenifer, Patsy, and Evan, go to the cellar and bring up all the turnips and onions you can carry.

"Danny, you find your father and tell him I need a good big piece of meat right away. Then fetch some more wood for the fire. I'm going to make enough stew to fill every kettle and pot in the house so that we can give those poor men something to eat when they arrive."

She bustled about the kitchen, sending all the children on errands so quickly that they had no chance to ask questions about the news that the officer had brought. The minute Danny returned with the wood she gave him the names of the five ladies who had been invited to sew, and sent him off to tell them that the quilting bee had been postponed. Then she asked Gil to bring more water and told the girls to peel the onions and turnips.

Uncle Benjamin brought in the meat, and by the time Danny had returned from his round of errands, fragrant stew was simmering over the fire and Aunt Abigail and the girls were mixing a great batch of buckwheat batter.

"We're going to make buckwheat cakes," Patsy told him, brushing back a stray lock of hair with a floury finger. "There isn't nearly enough bread because tomorrow is baking day."

Jenifer interrupted her. "Did you see any soldiers?" she asked.

Danny shook his head. "Only the lieutenant who was here this noon and four men with him," he said. "They are going around the village writing with chalk on the doors of the houses where the generals are to stay. I saw 'General Varnum's Quarters' written on the door of the Stephens' house, and 'General Huntington's Quarters' down on Zachary Davis' front door. I wish we were going to have a general at our house."

He looked at his mother. "If you don't need us any more, Mum, Gil and I can go to the crossroads and watch for the army," he suggested. "We'll come back and let you know the very minute we see the soldiers coming."

Aunt Abigail, who was shaking flour into the tub of batter, thought this a very good idea. So Gil hastily put on his heavy jacket and pulled his woolen cap well over his ears. Then the two boys went off, each boasting to the other as they ran along the icy road that he would be the first to hear

Eleven Thousand Hungry Men

the drums and fifes and to see the flags of the approaching army.

It was nearly dark when they came back, bursting into the kitchen and leaving the door swinging wide open behind them. Their coats and caps were thickly powdered with snow. They were cold. And they were almost speechless with dismay, surprise, and lack of breath.

"Men!" Gil gasped in a voice so choked that Jenifer thought he was going to cry. "Hundreds of them coming along the road. But it can't be the army, Aunt Abigail! It can't be! An army doesn't look like that. I've seen the militia march in Phila——" He stopped to draw a breath and quickly Danny took up the story.

"They haven't any uniforms and their feet are bleeding and there aren't any drums and they——" He clutched miserably at his father's arm. "Oh, they are in a sorry state. Come and help them! Please come and help them!"

"I'm coming!" Uncle Benjamin said. Dropping the ax helve which he had been carving, he snatched up his greatcoat and ran out of the house with the two boys close at his heels. At the gate he stopped

Silver for General Washington

and whistled under his breath when he saw the column of ragged, weary men which was approaching.

They were not marching. With their muskets over their shoulders, they were dragging along at a snail's pace often stumbling, falling, and struggling to their feet, to go on again. Some wore shoes that were cracked open and full of holes. Others shuffled along with their feet wrapped in rags. Still others picked their way barefooted over the icy road, leaving bloody footprints in the snow.

Except for a word of encouragement now and then for the men who had stumbled, they pushed ahead silently. Fully two hundred of them had shuffled past the Gardners' house when shouted commands brought the column to a halt. One of the big guns along the line had slipped into the ditch by the roadside, and the soldiers who were harnessed to it needed help in pulling it out.

Some of the men dropped to the ground at once to rest. Others stood about blowing on their hands and beating their arms against their bodies, trying to get warm. A young officer with a captain's cockade in his soiled three-cornered hat had

Eleven Thousand Hungry Men

stopped near the gate. Uncle Benjamin spoke to him in an undertone.

"We have food in the kitchen if your men are hungry," he said.

"Hungry!" exclaimed the captain. "We're starving. How many can you feed?"

"Twenty-five or thirty," Uncle Benjamin replied. "I wish it were the whole army."

"Good Lord, sir, so do I," the captain said. "Most of my men have had nothing but frozen potatoes, dry corn, and a few shreds of salt beef for the last three days. Please wait a minute."

He turned to a lieutenant who stood nearby and the two held a whispered conversation. Then thirty names were called out and, one after another, thirty soldiers stepped from the ranks and followed Uncle Benjamin and the boys to the rear of the house.

A moment later the warm, candle-lighted kitchen was filled with tired, ragged, hungry men, who crowded as close to the fire as they could, and grasped eagerly at the dishes filled with steaming stew which Aunt Abigail and the girls handed them. They ate greedily, gulping down the hot food hastily, and sopping up every drop of gravy with the buckwheat cakes baked that afternoon.

When the last spoonful of stew had been scraped from the pots and the last cake had disappeared, they left, jostling each other good-naturedly as they went out of the door and calling back their thanks. The army had just begun to move forward when they stepped into the ranks. Gil and Danny, who had followed the soldiers to the gate, could

Eleven Thousand Hungry Men

see no end to the long, slowly advancing column.

It was not until the vanguard had reached Valley Creek that the order came down the line to break ranks and make camp. Then like ants the weary soldiers spread out over the hills and meadows of Valley Forge.

Hundreds of them dropped their muskets and sprawled on the snowy earth to rest their aching feet. But others set to work chopping down trees and tearing apart fences for firewood. Several farmers protested when they saw their fence rails being destroyed. But their protests did little good, for the freezing soldiers were determined to waste no time in starting blazes big enough to warm their shivering bodies and to cook what little food they had.

For a short while Gil and Danny watched the fires starting up all over the fields and meadows, and listened to the men calling back and forth as they searched for water and wood. Then, although soldiers were still straggling past the house in a steady stream, the two boys hurried inside, for an icy wind was tossing the bare branches of the trees and the snow was falling fast.

CHAPTER EIGHT

Something Strange Afoot

GIL WAS cold. Still half-asleep, he moved closer to Danny and reached out to pull up the heavy quilt which usually lay at the foot of the bed. It was not there, and as he drew his arm back under the bedclothes he remembered what had become of it. Only the previous afternoon Aunt Abigail had gathered together every blanket and quilt which could possibly be spared from each bed, put them all into a pile, and announced to her family that they were going to be given to the soldiers.

"We can sleep in our clothes if we are cold, and these covers are going to warm men who have scarce any clothes at all," she said.

And she directed Danny and Gilbert to help her carry the blankets and quilts to the Quaker Meetinghouse, where a score of soldiers lay on beds of straw, ill with camp fever.

Something Strange Afoot

Gil shut his eyes for a minute remembering how strange the Meetinghouse had looked, with all the benches removed and sick men lying about on the floor, moaning and tossing. Then, although he knew it was still early, he climbed out of bed, snatched his clothes, and tiptoed quickly downstairs to the kitchen—the only warm room in the house.

Uncle Benjamin had been there before him on his way to the barn and had stirred up the fire which was blazing brightly. Gil hugged it as he dressed. At last, buttoning his jacket, he crossed the room to peer out of the window. The glass was so thickly frosted that he could not see through it.

Breathing on one of the panes, he rubbed it with his sleeve until he had a peephole. It had stopped snowing, but the sky was gray and filled with clouds. Down the road, about a half a mile away, smoke rose steadily from the chimneys of a row of little new log huts. And at the entrance of the lane which led to Zachary Davis' house, where General Huntington was staying, a picket was pacing back and forth.

"Maybe that's Seth," Gil thought. Turning to

Silver for General Washington

the fire he picked up a poker, felt around in the ashes at one end of the fireplace, and fished out a potato which he had saved from his supper the night before. It was crisp and burned black. But it was still hot and he knew that inside it was white and mealy. Slipping it into the pocket of his greatcoat, he pulled on the coat and his stocking cap.

Then he unfastened the heavy latch on the back door and stepped outside. It was so cold that his breath came out like little puffs of smoke, and the snow crunched under his feet as he ran down the path and started along the road in the direction of the picket.

Three weeks had passed since the American army had come to Valley Forge. They had been dreadful weeks for the soldiers. At daybreak on the morning after their arrival, all of the men who were strong enough to work had been ordered to start at once to build shelters. Swirling snow drifted against their legs and stung their bare chapped hands and faces as they chopped down trees on the neighboring hillsides. Bitter winds blew through their ragged clothing as they hauled logs from the forests.

Something Strange Afoot

Yet they kept steadily at work, and, one after another, nearly nine hundred new huts—all built alike and standing in rows in various parts of the village—had been finished. Now at last every soldier in camp had some protection from the cruel weather. And George Washington, who had refused to seek warm quarters for himself until his men were provided for, had finally left his big tent, which had been pitched on the hill near the school, and moved into the sturdy stone house, not far from the ruined forge, which he had rented from Mrs. Deborah Hewes.

Several times Gil had seen the tall Commander in Chief riding his big gray horse about the encampment and talking earnestly with the generals who rode beside him. And only the other day Seth had told Gil that if it were not for General Washington he would leave the army and go back home.

"We're freezin' and we're starvin' but there's somethin' about the General that holds us to him, and I couldn't tell you what it is no more than I could fly," Seth had said.

Seth called himself a Yankee and told Gil that he came from a place to the north named Connect-

Silver for General Washington

icut. It was on the sixth day after the arrival of the army that he and Gil had met.

Gil and Danny had been walking home from the Stephens' house when they had come upon an an old soldier sitting by the roadside in the snow. His coat was tattered, with both sleeves split at the elbows. His breeches were worn so thin that one bare blue knee showed through. The cockade on his three-cornered hat drooped forlornly over one ear.

Altogether he had seemed the picture of misery as he squatted in the snow, tightening some rags which were wrapped around his feet. But when the boys stopped to talk with him he answered them jokingly, and looked up at them with a pair of the friendliest eyes Gil had ever seen.

During the rest of the day Gil had thought often about the soldier. And the following morning without telling anybody what he was about, he had stuffed some woolen stockings into his jacket pocket, hidden his second pair of shoes under his greatcoat, and set out in search of him.

He had found Seth near the half-finished Connecticut huts, melting some snow over the camp-

Something Strange Afoot

fire for drinking water. "Lord love you, lad, I ain't much taller than you are, I know, but I couldn't do more than get my big toes into those things," he declared with a grin when Gil showed him the stockings and shoes.

"Try," Gil urged.

So, squatting in the snow, Seth had pulled on the long stockings and squeezed on the shoes. And after he had eased his feet by cutting slits in each shoe so that his toes stuck out, he chuckled and announced that he had not been so warm and comfortable since he had lost his own boots after the battle of Brandywine Creek.

Now Seth and Gil were good friends. The people of Valley Forge were allowed to go and come as they pleased about the camp, and Gil had been several times to the hut which Seth shared with eleven other soldiers. And as often as he could, he took food along, for he had discovered that Seth, like all the other men in the encampment, was always hungry.

Eleven thousand soldiers had struggled through the snow to Valley Forge on that bitter night of December the nineteenth. Eleven thousand men

Silver for General Washington

who brought with them almost nothing to eat. Snow and then more snow had blocked the narrow roads leading to the village. Except for some salt herring and a very small quantity of fresh meat, few supplies had reached the camp. The army storehouses were now empty of everything but flour—and there were not many barrels of that. For the past two days the soldiers had had nothing to eat but tasteless cakes, made of flour and water and baked on flat stones near their fires.

Loyal neighboring farmers had already given or sold to the army all the meat, eggs, milk, and grain that they could spare and their wives had fed the hungry men who came begging to their doors. But the supplies which the farmers had laid by for the winter were fast disappearing. Already the Gardners' springhouse, cellar, smokehouse, and storeroom were more than half-empty. Bessie's calf had been killed to make a meal for some soft-spoken soldiers from the faraway state of North Carolina. Not a pig was left in the pigsty. And only three chickens now came cackling to the kitchen steps when Patsy fed them their scraps each day.

"We won't have enough to keep ourselves and

Something Strange Afoot

the children alive until spring if we give anything else away," Aunt Abigail had told Uncle Benjamin at the supper table the night before. And she had looked so worried that Gil had not asked her for anything extra for Seth, but had slipped his own potato into his lap and hidden it later in the ashes.

Now as he ran along the road he thought how pleased Seth would be when he sank his teeth through the blackened skin. He was disappointed when he found that the soldier on duty was a man he did not know.

"Where's Seth?" he asked, running along beside the sentry, who was still pacing back and forth.

The soldier chuckled and leaned on his musket. "His breeches give out," he drawled. "Split right down the back, they did, just as he was startin' to come out, and he didn't have nothin' under 'em nor nothin' to put over 'em, so I took his spell a while till he gets 'em mended. What do you want with him anyway?"

"Just to give him this." Gil fished the potato from his pocket. Then his face fell as he turned it over in his hand. "Aw, thunder, it's stone cold!" he exclaimed.

Silver for General Washington

"No matter, bub. Ain't nothin' will stay hot on a day such as this 'un, and hot or cold it will slip down just as easy," the soldier said. And he eyed the potato so hungrily that Gil thrust it into his hand.

"Eat it," the boy blurted out. "I'll get something else for Seth."

Then, because it gave him a queer feeling to see how eagerly the half-starved man wolfed down the cold, blackened potato, Gil turned and ran for home as fast as he could go.

The family was already up and everyone except Evan was dressed when he entered the kitchen. Breakfast of porridge and slices of rye bread spread with apple butter was soon ready and quickly over. There was no need now for the children to rush off to school, for the schoolhouse had been turned into a hospital shortly after the arrival of the army. But there was plenty for all of them to do. The girls set to work to help Aunt Abigail clear away the breakfast dishes and put the kitchen to rights, while Danny and Gil pulled on their coats and started out to fill the woodbox. As they reached the door, however, Aunt Abigail called them back.

"As soon as you have finished your chores I

Something Strange Afoot

want you to go to Widow Johnson's," she said. "She has been ransacking her garret, the same as we have, looking for old clothes, and like as not she'll have found some that can be fixed up for those poor lads down the road. Get her bundle first. Then go across the river to Mrs. Maddock's and ask her if she has any clothing she can spare. Fetch whatever they give you straight home so that I can start mending and patching at once."

At the name "Maddock," Uncle Benjamin, who was sitting near the fire putting on his boots, had looked up sharply. But he said nothing as he picked up a piece of harness which he had been mending and went outside. Later on, however, when the boys were starting out on their errands, he motioned to them from the barn door.

"Look sharp when you are over across the river," he said in an undertone. "I didn't want to fret your mother with this because Mrs. Maddock is her friend, but there was talk in Slab Tavern last night that makes me think Tom Maddock will bear watching."

Danny whistled softly in surprise.
"What kind of talk?"

Silver for General Washington

"Just talk," his father replied shortly. "If there's truth in it I'll tell you later. If there's not there would be only harm in repeating it. All I want you to do is to keep your eyes open while you are in Tom Maddock's house and let me know if you see anything out of the way."

Both boys nodded soberly. A moment later they set off together across the snowy fields. Mrs. Johnson's house was not far away, but the house of Thomas Maddock and his wife was set some distance back from the opposite bank of the Schuylkill River and it was nearly noon before Gil and Danny reached home again. Gil carried a pair of shabby leather breeches, while Danny had a homespun skirt bundled under his arm and several badly worn, unmatched woolen stockings stuffed into his greatcoat pocket.

Aunt Abigail exclaimed with satisfaction as the boys laid the clothing before her.

"I can patch up the breeches and make a good warm shirt out of this skirt," she said. Then, picking up the woolen stockings, she held them out to Jenifer and Patsy, who had come to see what the boys had brought.

Something Strange Afoot

"Here, Jen, you and Patsy can start unraveling these right after dinner. We'll dye the yarn with some of that sassafras bark you gathered last fall and then knit up stockings as good as new." She turned to Danny. "Which clothes did Hannah Maddock send?" she asked.

"She didn't send any," Danny answered, spreading his hands to the fire. "We knocked and knocked but there wasn't anybody home." Then, trying to hide the excitement in his voice, he inquired, "Where's Pa?"

"Still out in the barn," his mother replied. "Isaac Walker has just sent word that there's a wagonload of straw upset in the snow out past Perkiomen Creek. It's needed sorely for the soldiers to sleep on and your father is going to try to bring some in. He says the roads are so bad he's going to travel on the river and he's hitching old Peg to the sleigh."

Danny turned to Gil. "Let's go and help him," he said, and he let himself out of the back door with Gil close behind him.

The boys found Uncle Benjamin fastening the last buckle on Peg's harness. The old horse stood with drooping head, switching her tail slowly back and forth. She did not look very sprightly, but the Gardners knew that they were lucky to have her.

Almost all of the neighboring farmers had been robbed of their horses by the Hessians or redcoats, or else they had turned them over to the American

Something Strange Afoot

army. Uncle Benjamin had lent his big grays and his heavy wagon to haul military supplies and had no idea when they would be returned to him. Only because of her age had he kept old Peg. And even as he hitched her up he was thinking sadly that her days of usefulness were nearly over and that he ought to shoot her.

"The hay she eats each day would feed one of those starving army horses, and her hide would make shoes for the soldiers," he told himself.

Yet he said nothing of his thoughts as he lifted his head to speak to the boys. Already Danny had begun to explain in a loud whisper how the Maddocks' house had been shut up tight.

"Even the barn was locked!" Danny exclaimed. "But there's something strange afoot all right, 'cause on the way home we crossed the river at Catfish Island and there was Mr. Maddock, kind of half-hidden by that big buttonwood tree, talking with a man I've never seen before."

The boy stopped to draw breath and his father asked quickly, "What did the stranger look like?"

"Well, he was old," Danny replied, "and tall, and——"

"And he was sort of bent over," Gil interrupted eagerly. "And he carried a cane. We couldn't see his face, but he had his queue tied up in a snakeskin bag, and just when we were passing he was taking something from Mr. Maddock that looked like a piece of paper all folded up."

"Did you hear anything either of the men was saying?" Uncle Benjamin asked.

Gil and Danny shook their heads.

"Well, keep your eyes open and your mouths shut, both of you, and if ever you come on him again around in these parts let me know at once," Uncle Benjamin told them. He climbed into the sleigh. "Danny, tell your mother I likely won't be back until dark and ask her to keep something hot for me," he said, and picking up the reins he clucked to Peg.

The old horse strained at the traces and the sleigh moved slowly forward, its runners squeaking in the snow. Gil and Danny watched until Uncle Benjamin had turned it toward the river. Then Danny shut the barn door and, still talking and wondering about Mr. Maddock and the stranger, the boys crossed the yard and went into the house.

Something Strange Afoot

The kitchen smelled of cooking and Jenifer was putting plates filled with sausage, sauerkraut, and boiled onions on the table. Gil sniffed hungrily as he sat down to dinner. He measured his piece of sausage with his eyes. He would eat one third of it, he thought. Then when he had a chance he would wrap the rest in his handkerchief and slip it into his pocket for Seth. This would have to be done when Aunt Abigail was not looking, for lately she had begun to insist that the children eat every morsel which she put upon their plates.

Before the meal was half-over the chance came which Gil hoped for. In answer to a knock at the door Danny let in two soldiers who said they had been sent to collect dirty tallow. This would be mixed with wood ashes to make soap which was badly needed in the camp. It was while Aunt Abigail was getting together all the tallow she could spare that Gil slid the sausage from his plate. And shortly after the meal was over he set out for the second time that day with food in his pocket for Seth.

CHAPTER NINE

Gil Finds and Loses a Friend

THERE WAS so little light in the hut that Seth could hardly see what he was doing. He hitched his three-legged stool closer to the fire. Squinting his eyes, he stuck his tongue between his teeth, and with his hunting knife he slowly carved a line on the cow horn which was grasped firmly in his left hand. Then he looked up.

"How do you spell 'sure,' Tom?" he asked.

The man called Tom laid down the snowshoe he was making and shook his head.

"I don't know. I ain't never had no schoolin'. Ask Davey," he said, motioning toward a quiet figure which lay stretched out on one of the built-in bunks on the opposite side of the room.

"Can't," Seth replied. "The poor lad's sleepin' at last an' I don't want to rouse him."

"That's right." A third man, with a blanket

Gil Finds and Loses a Friend

wrapped around his shoulders and a cocked hat on the back of his head looked up from the musket which he was cleaning. "Davey's leg is swole up the size of a sack of flour, and it don't pain him so much when he's sleepin'. Let him rest. I'll spell it out for you, Seth." He coughed and scratched his head thoughtfully. "S—h—" he drawled, "u—r—e."

Seth repeated the letters after him. "S—h—u—r—e. Thankee, Caleb," he said, and he began painstakingly to trace the word.

"What are you doin'?" Tom asked him after a few minutes had passed.

"Fancyin' up my powder horn," Seth said. "Look here." With a lean finger he pointed proudly to the words which he had scratched in shaky letters around the rim of the horn.

*"The redcoat who steels this horn
Will go to hel as shure's he's born."*

Seth read them aloud slowly. "That'll be real nice when I've got it carved deep, won't it?" he asked.

Tom nodded. "It'll look good," he said, and went back to stringing his snowshoe.

Silver for General Washington

For some time the three men worked on in silence. The heavy breathing of the sleeping Davey and the crackling of the fire were the only sounds in the room. Once a burning log fell apart, sending a shower of sparks up the chimney, and the fire blazed up. The dancing flames cast strange shadows on the wall. They lighted up the earthen floor, gleamed on a pewter cup which stood on the crude plank table, picked out the red patch in the tattered shirt hanging in the corner, and shone on the thin, worn faces of the soldiers.

Suddenly the door was thrust open, letting in a blast of icy air. A young man with a fur cap on his head, but no coat over his ragged jacket, entered. He set his musket on the buckhorns over the fireplace and squatted down beside Seth.

"I've hauled so many sledgeloads of wood that the rope's cut my hands near in two," he said, spreading out his fingers. "It's God's pity they can't get feed enough around here to keep the horses alive. The poor creatures are dying off like flies."

Tom looked at him and scowled. "What you a-chewin' on, Henry?" he demanded.

Gil Finds and Loses a Friend

"Bark off a little birch tree," Henry replied with a grin. "I wouldn't want my teeth to forget what they are for, would I?"

Tom grunted. "Mine are fallin' out with not being used," he muttered, standing up to try his snowshoe. "I'm goin' to take me off to a place where there's somethin' for 'em to work on."

Seth swung around on his stool. "What do you mean, Tom?" he asked sharply.

"Mean what I say," Tom replied. "I've starved, an' I've friz, an' I've marched, an' I've pulled loads like I was a pack horse long enough. My enlistment time is up Thursday an I'm goin' home where a man can live decent."

Seth laid his cow horn on the dirt floor and rose.

"You can't do that, Tom," he said, peering up into the tall man's face. "You've got to fight some more. Don't you know it ain't possible to live decent in a country where some blasted king miles across the ocean is tellin' you, 'Do this an' don't you dare do that'? You can't live decent unless you're free—unless you can kind of be your own king and have a say-so in makin' the laws you got to live under."

Silver for General Washington

He put his hand on Tom's arm. "Don't leave us, Tom," he pleaded. "We all enlisted together. Our time is near up too, Henry's and Davey's and Caleb's and mine. But we ain't runnin' home. We're stickin'. Ain't that right, Caleb?"

Caleb rubbed his musket barrel with the flat of his hand. "That's right," he said slowly. "It takes strong men like us to fight a war. Only the chicken-hearted ones dribble away when their enlistment time is up, or go sneakin' out of the camp at night, like Andy and Jerry, desertin' the cause they signed up to fight for."

Tom shook his shaggy black head slowly like an angry bear.

"Don't you name me in the same breath with them deserters," he growled. "I'd stay an' fight if there was any use. But there ain't. First place, the redcoats are gettin' fat as pigs and all rested up there in Philadelphia while we're freezin' an' starvin' here. Second place, we can't win a war if we don't all fight it together. An' how in tarnation can we all fight together when we're fightin' each other all the time? Why, those drawlin' Virginians hates us Yankees same as we hate them. An' I wouldn't trust

Gil Finds and Loses a Friend

no man from New Jersey nor Pennsylvania, not even with my old, good-for-nothin' breeches."

"But you must trust 'em," Seth said earnestly. "Don't you see it ain't right any more to talk about Virginians an' Pennsylvanians an' Jersey men? We're all kind of hitched up together now. We're Americans—and we're all fightin' for the same thing—liberty."

"That's a fine-soundin' word," Tom declared. "If I——" He broke off. "Harkee!" he exclaimed. "There's someone wants to get in." And pushing Seth aside, he strode across the room and pulled open the slab door so suddenly that Gil, who was standing on the threshold, tumbled into the hut and landed on his knees on the floor.

Tom chuckled. "Try comin' in on your feet next time, young feller," he advised, and pushed the door shut quickly.

Gil's cheeks were crimson as he scrambled to his feet. Pulling the sausage from his pocket he stuck it out toward Seth.

The old soldier's eyes brightened. "Look, the lad's brought us a bit of meat!" he exclaimed. "Wait till I cut it and I'll give you each a piece."

Silver for General Washington

He laid the sausage on the bare table and cut it into five thin slices. Quickly Tom and Henry each reached for his share, but Caleb went on cleaning his musket and made no move in the direction of the table.

"What's the matter, Caleb?" Seth asked anxiously, spearing a slice of sausage with his knife and holding it out to his friend. "Don't you want none?"

Caleb shook his head. "You can keep my share for Davey. I'm not feeling so spry," he confessed, reaching inside his shirt to scratch his chest. "If I could take me a good wash-off I'd feel better, maybe. Seems like I ain't had the touch of hot water on me for a year of Sundays."

"Wait till the ice breaks on the river. You'll have more water than you need then," Tom advised, licking the last bit of sausage from his fingers and rubbing his hands on his breeches. He turned to pick up his snowshoe and his mouth fell open. "Now, what in tarnation are you up to, you young loblolly?" he asked, staring at Henry. "Have you gone crazed in the head like poor Reuben?"

Gil, who had been watching Henry, wondered,

Gil Finds and Loses a Friend

too, if the young soldier had taken leave of his senses. For Henry had carefully covered one end of the table with the shirt which had hung in the corner of the hut and had laid his slice of sausage on a bark-slab plate. Now, pulling a stool to the table, he sat down, took a two-pronged fork from his jacket pocket, picked up Seth's hunting knife and began to carve his sliver of meat delicately into tiny bits.

Of all the men in the room only Seth seemed to know what Henry was doing.

Leaning his elbows on the table and peering up into Henry's face, with twinkling blue eyes, he asked, "And how's your dinner, my lad?"

Henry winked. "Excellent," he replied, lifting a morsel of sausage to his mouth. "This thick, juicy roast of beef is so tender it melts on my tongue. And the gravy! Umm! It's rich and red and steaming hot. As for the warm bread and the apple pie, they are——" Suddenly he dropped his fork and lifted his arm to shield his head.

With hand raised high Tom stood over him, his eyes blazing.

"Don't mock us!" he shouted. "Don't mock us.

Silver for General Washington

I can't stand to hear no more blatherin' about food."

Seth grabbed the angry man by the arm.

"Hush, you'll wake Davey," he warned.

Looking somewhat ashamed of his outburst, Tom dropped his hand and turned away. But the damage had been done. The figure on the bunk stirred. Davey groaned, raised himself on his elbow and looked around. His eyes were bright and his cheeks blazed with fever.

"They're still shooting," he said wildly. "Hear them! It's the redcoats—and I've lost my musket.

Gil Finds and Loses a Friend

You, there——" He looked straight at Gil. "You—help me find my musket. Help——" He swung one foot over the side of the bunk, then sank back on the straw.

"Oh, my leg," he moaned. "My leg. It pains me sore. Can't someone stop the paining?"

Caleb had sprung to his feet when Davey first moved. Now he bent over the young soldier as tenderly as a woman.

"Hush, lad," he begged. "Lie quiet." He put his hand on Davey's forehead and turned to Seth. "He's burnin' up, he is, worse than he was this morning. Will you help me carry him to the hospital?"

Seth shook his head hopelessly. "There ain't no use. Every hospital in camp's so crowded that the men are lyin' most on top of each other. We'd do better just to keep him quiet-like till we can get the surgeon's mate tonight to bleed him."

But keeping Davey quiet was something that no one seemed able to do. Out of his head with fever, he twisted and tossed, so determined to get up that it took both Seth and Caleb to hold him. Even when Henry laid his musket beside him he was not content, but insisted that it was not his and that it would not shoot.

Seth turned to Henry in despair. "Let's try singin'," he said. "He always likes singin'." And in a voice that quavered and squeaked he began softly:

> "*The day is broke, my boys, push on*
> *And follow, follow Washington.*
> *'Tis he that leads the way.*"

One after another the other men joined in the chorus. Even Tom hung over the bunk, humming along with the rest.

> "*'Tis he that leads the way.*
> *When he commands we will obey,*
> *Through rain or snow, by night or day,*
> *Determined to be free.*
> *Determined to be free.*"

On they went through that verse and the next. Still Davey tossed and struggled.

"That ain't doin' no good," Seth decided at last. "Seems to make him worse." Then looking sadly at Gil, who had come to stand at the foot of the bunk, he added, " 'Tis a pity there ain't no one can

Gil Finds and Loses a Friend

play him a tune on that fiddle of his. That would quiet him sure."

"Fiddle," Gil echoed, hardly believing his ears. "I can play on a fiddle. Where is it?"

"In that box yonder." Seth motioned with his head to a big box which stood against the end wall of the hut.

In an instant Gil crossed the room and lifted the lid. There wrapped in an old red flannel petticoat lay a fiddle and bow. Carefully Gil unwrapped them. Then he gasped. His breath came quickly and his hand shook a little as he carried the fiddle close to the fire and peered at it intently. A great wave of happiness swept over him. Joyfully he straightened up and turned to the men.

"Why, it's my——" he began. But something in Seth's worried eyes and his quick command, "Play, go on, play," stopped him. Choking back the words that had rushed to his lips, he tucked the fiddle under his chin and drew the bow lovingly across the strings.

He had not been so happy in weeks. But his mind was in a turmoil. What did it mean? Here in his hands, here under his chin, was his own fiddle.

There was no doubt about it. He could tell by the way it looked. He could tell by the way it felt—by the way it sounded—by the little scratch across the neck which he had made on it accidentally when it was new. His own fiddle that a Hessian soldier had stolen. And now it belonged to a soldier named Davey.

He was so bewildered that he could think of nothing to play but he softly tried a few notes. Then as he tightened a string he remembered a song which his father had taught him several years earlier and he began it haltingly at first and then with a surer touch. He had finished the piece and played a long, slow hymn before poor Davey

Gil Finds and Loses a Friend

seemed to hear the music. But gradually, as Gil went on through all the pieces he had learned, the young soldier grew quiet. One by one, Henry, Tom, and Caleb left the bunk and sat down close to the fire. At last even Seth turned away.

"That's done it, lad," he said with a tired smile. "He's sleepin'. But keep on playin'. I notice you kind of trip over some of your notes now and then, but it sounds real good."

Gil leaned against the table, racking his brains for one last tune that he could play, and began the slow measures of a piece by Handel. When he had finished it seemed for an instant as though the music had cast a spell over the room, for no one moved or spoke.

But the spell was broken suddenly when a great gust of wind swooped down the chimney, sending out a shower of ashes and sparks and filling the room with thick, acrid smoke. Sputtering and coughing, Caleb and Henry sprang up to stamp out the sparks. With an oath, Tom grabbed a blanket from one of the bunks and went outside. Seth stood up, his eyes streaming from the smoke, and took the violin from Gil's hands.

Silver for General Washington

"I'll put it away careful for him," he said, wrapping the red flannel petticoat around the violin and laying it in the box. "He thinks more of this fiddle than he does of livin', Davey does."

"Oh," Gil said flatly, wiping the smoke-tears away from his eyes. "Where—where did he get it?"

Seth closed down the lid of the box.

"We found it a-layin' in a barn near Germantown, right after we fought the redcoats there," he said, straightening up. "There Davey was a-grievin' an' a-frettin' an' a-wishin' he had brought his own fiddle from home, when Caleb felt somethin' in the straw and pulled out this. It was like a miracle. An' good luck for us, too. Many's the cold night when Davey's livened us up with a tune, an' kept us from thinkin' on our troubles."

"Oh!" Gil said again. "But it's—I mean, you see, once I had——" He swallowed hard. "I mean it's time for me to go home," he choked, managing a feeble grin. "I'll be back tomorrow, maybe." And limping quickly across the hut he let himself out.

"Bravely and well, no matter how difficult.

Gil Finds and Loses a Friend

Bravely and well, no matter how difficult." The words from his father's letter sang themselves through his mind like a song, as he made his way down the snowy road toward home.

He hadn't done it very well, he thought. He hadn't done it very bravely. He hadn't even intended to do it at all. But it had been difficult—the most difficult thing he had ever done in his life—giving up his violin which he loved so dearly and could so easily have claimed.

"It's done now," he told himself soberly, plunging his hands deep into his greatcoat pockets. "I could never take it away now. And I'll never tell anyone as long as I live that it's my violin lying in Davey's box. Never."

It was dusk and the snow had begun again. As Gil turned off Baptist Road where the Connecticut huts stood a bitter wind met him. Whistling and sighing, it blew his breath back into his body and blinded him with fine white snowflakes. Pulling his cap down farther over his ears he lowered his head and pushed on.

Except for six soldiers who were pulling a heavy sledge loaded with firewood, the road was empty.

Silver for General Washington

Some horses stood with drooping heads before Dr. Stephens' house where General Varnum had his headquarters. As Gil drew near the house, the door was opened and three men stepped out. The tallest, a man with a cape over his shoulders, led the way quickly down the path, loosened the rein by which his horse was tied, and sprang into the saddle.

"Good night to you, Varnum," Gil heard him call in a strong voice. "I'll talk with you tomorrow on that matter of shoes." Then he reined his horse around.

"It's General Washington," Gil thought and he stepped to the side of the road to get out of the General's way.

From his seat on his great gray horse the Commander in Chief looked down at the boy and smiled.

"It's a cold evening, lad, for you to be out," he said. "Better hasten home before the storm grows worse."

"Yes, sir," Gil stammered. "I will."

He did not know why but for some reason a warm feeling of comfort had stolen over him at the sound of the General's voice. The loss of his

Gil Finds and Loses a Friend

violin for the second time did not seem quite so hard to bear as he watched General Washington and his companions ride on until a curtain of snow hid them from sight, and he whistled softly as he turned his face to the wind again and plodded on.

Night was falling rapidly now. By the time Gil passed the lane leading to General Huntington's headquarters, it was so dark that he could barely see the sentinel on duty. The shivering man had tied a scarf around his head and was standing in his cocked hat, in order to protect his rag-wrapped feet from the frozen, snow-covered ground.

It was so dark as Gil neared home that the candles which Jenifer had placed in the window made little golden pools of light on the snow. It was so dark when at last he turned in at the gate, hurrying to reach the warmth of the kitchen, that he did not notice the man who had been walking not far behind him, and who now passed on down the road toward Philadelphia—the man with his queue in a snakeskin bag.

CHAPTER TEN

A Daring Plan

IT HAD been raining hard since early morning. Rain beat against the walls of the huts where men who had not been able for weeks to drill or parade because of bad weather, sat huddled close to their fires. It played a noisy tune on the roofs of the little hospitals scattered here and there throughout the encampment where other men groaned and tossed, or lay quiet, too ill to move.

It trickled down the necks of the sentries, as they stood on platforms in the highest branches of the tallest trees in camp, keeping watch lest the redcoats should leave their snug quarters in Philadelphia and attack Valley Forge. It seeped through the thin clothing and worn shoes of the pickets, pacing back and forth at their posts. And it ran in steady rivers down the little panes of the kitchen window of the Gardners' house.

A Daring Plan

Yet the kitchen itself was warm and snug. Close to the fire Aunt Abigail was sewing, taking in the waistband of Patsy's pink-and-white-striped shortgown and worrying because lately all the children had been growing too thin for their clothes. Sprawled on the floor at her feet Evan was looking contentedly at the pictures in Gil's copy of Foxe's *Book of Martyrs*. And at the table behind her Jenifer, Patsy, Gilbert, and Danny were doing their lessons.

" 'Tis a pity that the children should forget all they have learned just because the school is closed," Aunt Abigail had told Uncle Benjamin several days earlier. "There is small use in fighting for the freedom of a country where the boys and girls are allowed to grow up as dunces. You set lessons for the boys each night, Benjamin, and whenever I can spare the time I will see that they do them, and that they help Jenifer and Patsy to read and to spell."

So it had been arranged. And every afternoon since then Aunt Abigail had managed to find two hours when, under her watchful eye, all four children studied their books and tried to improve their handwriting. Now Patsy and Jenifer were copying sentences in their brown paper copybooks, and Danny was struggling with a sum his father had set for him. But Gil was idle. Chewing absentmindedly on the tip of his goose-quill pen, he sat with his book lying open before him, staring out of the window.

He was thinking not of his lessons, but of Seth and Davey, Caleb and Henry and Tom. He was remembering the visit which he had made to the hut the day before, when he had taken some bread to Davey, who was now almost well. He was seeing in his mind the lean, pale faces of his soldier friends, and he seemed to hear their voices as they had talked together.

Things were still going badly for Seth and his companions. In fact, after eight long weeks in Valley Forge, things were in a sorry state throughout the entire camp. The army was smaller and weaker now. Many men who were worried about their families, or tired of hardship and hunger, had marched home when their enlistment periods were up. Many others had deserted. Hundreds had died of disease or starvation. And those who remained were still starving, ragged, and cold.

Again and again George Washington had written to the Continental Congress, which was meeting now in the little town of York, begging for help for his army. But no help had come.

"They have forgot us, that's what they have," Caleb had mourned, as Gil had sat in the hut the previous morning. "They have forgot us, and there's not a man in the country cares a hoot what becomes of us."

Silver for General Washington

"That ain't so, you old fuss-and-feathers," Seth had declared bluntly, grunting as he pushed a big needle through the heavy cloth of a jacket he was darning. "The General cares what happens to us, don't he? Else why would he ride around the camp like he does, visitin' in our huts and offerin' us words of hope and cheer?"

Henry, who sat on a log near the fire, looked up from the book which he was reading and smiled.

"You can't eat hope and cheer, Seth," he reminded the old soldier. "But it's God's truth that the General does the best for us that's in his power. What he needs to run this war is money—good hard money—and if he doesn't get it soon it looks like the redcoats may lick us after all, and send us whimpering home with our tails between our legs."

Little else had then been said in the hut before Gil had left. And all the way home the boy had thought about Henry's words. He was still thinking of them as he now stared out at the rain, with Cocker's *Arithmetick* lying open, unheeded, on the table before him. And somehow all mixed up with Henry's words were words which his father had written in the letter which Gil had almost

A Daring Plan

memorized before he had burned it. Gil wrinkled his forehead and bit harder on his pen as he tried to recall exactly what his father's letter had said.

"If you need money for anything important, remember . . . remember . . ."

Suddenly like a streak of lightning the rest of the sentence flashed into his head. And almost as suddenly a breath-taking plan popped into his mind. It was a simple plan, yet so daring that he wondered for a minute whether or not he could carry it through. But as he thought it over, step by step, he decided that he could, and he would, and furthermore that no one should stop him.

He could not discuss this plan with Aunt Abigail or Uncle Benjamin, for if they learned of it they would never let him attempt to carry it out. But it would be only fair to tell Jenifer about it, he thought. And perhaps he might even have to tell Danny and ask his help.

Glancing impatiently at the tall clock in the corner he saw that at least fifteen minutes must pass before lessons would be over for the day. This seemed a long time to wait. Aunt Abigail was even stricter than Mr. Haskell had been about whispering in study time, and was sure to give him an extra sum to do if she caught him at it. So he dipped his pen in the leather ink bottle which stood between himself and his sister and began to write a note in clear, round letters.

"Meet me in the barn when lessons are over," he wrote. "Bring Danny, but not Patsy or Evan."

Nudging Jenifer's elbow he shoved the page toward her. Jenifer read the message slowly. Then she raised puzzled eyes to her brother and nodded. When she bent over her copying again she wondered what Gil could have on his mind that made his eyes so shining and his face so serious.

Perhaps it was because of the rain that Aunt Abigail kept all four children at work longer than usual that afternoon, and then gave Patsy and Jenifer each a seam to sew. At any rate it was nearly dark before Jenifer was able to throw a shawl over her dress, whisper a few words to Danny, and then run out with him to the barn. They found Gil, waiting just inside the door which he had left partly open for them, and bursting with excitement.

"I thought you'd never come," he exclaimed

A Daring Plan

softly as Jenifer shook the raindrops from her hair. "Come back here." And he dragged them both to the rear of the stable, which was empty now except for two clucking hens and Bessie, who looked up at the children with soft brown eyes and then went on peacefully chewing her cud.

Quickly Gil began to unfold his plan. First he repeated the conversation which he had heard in the hut.

"So it's money that General Washington needs more than anything else," he announced. "He needs it right now, too, if our side is going to win this war—and I know how to help him get some."

"How?" Danny asked in an unbelieving tone of voice.

Gil turned excitedly to his sister. "You know, don't you, Jen? It's the things we buried in the cellar," he said. "Father told us to sell them if we needed money for anything important. Well, I'm going to go to Philadelphia to get them and then give them to General Washington to sell."

Jenifer gasped and stared at her brother in the half-darkness of the barn as though she thought he had taken leave of his senses.

Silver for General Washington

"But you can't, Gil," she protested. "Why, you can't even get into Philadelphia. The British are there and the pickets would never let you pass. They'd stop you and——"

Gil shook his head. "No, they wouldn't. Listen, Jen, I've thought it all out. The redcoats would never stop a boy who was bringing food to the city to sell. I'll take some loaves of bread or something else along with me and pretend I am going to the market place. As soon as I pass the pickets I'll go straight to our house and find a way to get in. Then I'll dig up the chest and——"

Jenifer broke in. "No, no, you mustn't do it," she wailed softly. "You'll be captured and they'll think you're a spy. Or one of those Hessians will shoot at you, or——"

"Oh, nothing like that will happen," Gil interrupted impatiently. "I'll be careful."

By this time Jenifer was blinking back tears, but she sounded quite cheerful as two very sensible thoughts occurred to her. "Why, you couldn't possibly dig up that big chest alone," she declared. "And how on earth do you think you could carry all those heavy candlesticks and things through the

A Daring Plan

streets and past the British sentries and then all the way back here?"

For a moment Gil looked dashed. "Well," he admitted, "I haven't figured that part of it out yet. But I can manage it somehow. I know I can. I thought maybe Danny would help." He glanced hopefully at his cousin.

Danny was chewing on a straw which he had picked up from the barn floor. He spat it out and scratched his head. "How were you figuring you'd get to Philadelphia?" he asked. "It's a goodish way."

"It's only twenty miles," Gil replied quickly. "We can walk there in two days and sleep in someone's barn at night. Maybe we could even steal a ride part way."

Danny considered this seriously, staring thoughtfully at the two chickens which were pecking around near his feet. Suddenly the plan seemed to appeal to him. He grinned at Gil. "We can take old Speckle along to sell at the market instead of bread," he said. "I'll wring her neck before she makes a squawk and plop her into a bag just when we're ready to start."

Silver for General Washington

At this Gil nodded joyfully, but Jenifer made a little noise of distress. "It's a foolhardy plan," she exclaimed. "You shouldn't go, either one of you. I'll——"

Gil grabbed her by the arms. "Jen, you wouldn't tell Aunt Abigail or Uncle Benjamin what we're planning, would you?" he asked anxiously. "Or Patsy or Evan either? They might give us away and then it would all be spoiled. We'd never be able to go."

"No, of course I wouldn't tell," Jen declared indignantly, "but . . ." Her voice trailed off and she sounded so worried and unhappy that Gil gave her a friendly little shake.

"Just think, Jen, it's for General Washington," he cried under his breath. "It's for Seth and Davey and all those poor men. It's something we can do for our country. Don't you remember what Father wrote? 'If either of you is ever able to help in this fight I know that you will——' "

" 'Do it bravely and well, no matter how hard it is,' " Jenifer finished, swallowing a lump in her throat. She made herself smile. "All right. I had forgot. Go, and I'll not say another word."

A Daring Plan

"Good girl," Gil exclaimed. "Now, hark a minute. We'll need some food to eat on the way. If Danny or I go poking around the cupboard Aunt Abigail will wonder what we're up to. But you can slip some bread and cheese under your apron when you clear away the supper dishes and hide it away for us. Will you do it?"

Jenifer nodded. At that moment Danny made a lunge for Speckle, caught her around the neck and let her go again.

"I was just practicing," he announced, rubbing his hands together and looking at Gil, while the outraged Speckle flapped her wings and ran clucking angrily to the farther end of the barn. "When do you reckon we'd better start, Gil?"

"Tomorrow morning if the rain stops," he replied, and limped to the barn door to look out. In a split second he was back. "Uncle Benjamin is home. He's just turning in at the gate," he whispered.

"Then we'd better slip back into the house, one at a time, before he sets Ma to wondering where we are," Danny said. "You go first." And he gave Jenifer a little shove.

Silver for General Washington

Pulling her shawl closely around her shoulders with one hand and picking up her skirts with the other, Jen ran through the slackening rain to the kitchen shed. There she shook out her dress and tucked some wet curls under her mobcap. Then, trying to look as though nothing unusual were in the air, she stepped into the kitchen. A moment later Gil came in with an armful of wood. Danny followed shortly afterwards, whistling loudly, and announcing that the rain was stopping and that he thought it was going to clear.

He was right. By the time the supper dishes had been cleared away, the stars were out. And as the family settled themselves by the fire for the evening, Jenifer managed to get a word with her brother.

"There's food under the pillow on your bed," she said softly. "I slipped upstairs with it when no one was looking."

Gil gave her a grateful smile. "Good," he whispered. "We'll need it tomorrow."

CHAPTER ELEVEN

Trapping a Spy

JENIFER woke with a start and sat up in bed. She held her breath wondering what had aroused her, and strained her ears to catch some little noise in the attic above her, or the sound of a footfall on the stairs outside her door.

She had had only a few more words alone with Gil the night before, just as they were all getting ready to go upstairs to bed.

"We'll creep out before daylight," Gil had told her as he touched her candle with a spill which he had lighted at the fire. "Danny killed Speckle before he left the barn and we're all ready to leave. Try to keep Aunt Abigail and Uncle Benjamin from finding out where we have gone for as long as you can."

Thinking suddenly that perhaps her part in Gil's plan would be as difficult as his, Jen had nodded and asked quickly, "How many days will you be away?"

"Four or five. Maybe not so long if we manage to get a ride either way," Gil had whispered. Then he had said "Good night," rather loudly and turned to take his own candle from the shelf over the fireplace.

Now as Jenifer pulled the patchwork quilt closer under her chin and watched the first gray fingers of light steal through the ruffled curtains at the window, she listened intently, hoping to hear some creak or whisper which would tell her that Gilbert and Danny were still in the house. But there was no sound. The mouse which had awakened her with its gnawing had scampered back to its hole, and the boys for whom she was listening were already a good mile from home and well outside the limits of the encampment.

Danny carried the dead hen in a bag over his shoulder. Gil's greatcoat pocket bulged with the packet of food which Jenifer had slipped under his pillow the night before. The day was very cold, with low-hanging clouds filling the sky. Nowhere on the road ahead were there any signs of life, and

Trapping a Spy

Danny wished heartily that he were safe at home, waiting for his mother to call him to a good breakfast of hot porridge and milk.

"Looks like more snow," he remarked, shifting his bag from one shoulder to the other.

"Feels like it too," Gil agreed. "It's so cold that my feet have forgot that they belong to me."

"Mine too," Danny said. "We'll come to the King of Prussia Inn soon. They'll let us stop in the kitchen to warm ourselves. They know my pa well."

Gil glanced up quickly. "Why, that's the very reason we can't stop," he exclaimed. "They'll ask us questions and try to turn us back."

Danny grinned rather sheepishly. "I had forgot that," he confessed. "Well, we can slip into the stable if no one's about and rest our feet and have a bite to eat. I'm fair starved."

Gil nodded and the two boys plodded on in silence. It was daylight when they reached the inn and stepped behind the trunk of a large oak tree to look over the situation. The tavern sign, with its picture of the King of Prussia dressed in a bright blue coat and riding a high-stepping, purple-tailed steed, was swinging back and forth in the wind.

Under the sign a brown horse stood tied to a hitching post. But except for the horse and a yellow cat, picking her way daintily along the icy path that led to the springhouse, there was no living thing in sight. Then a boy came out of the stable with a bucket in his hand, looked at the sky, scratched his head, and walked off toward the kitchen, leaving the stable door unlatched and partly open.

Danny waited until the boy had disappeared around the house. Then he exclaimed, "Now's our chance," and darted into the stable.

Gil followed quickly, pulling the door shut behind him. It was almost dark inside the stable, but there was light enough so that the boys could see the horses in their stalls. Near the door was a dusty ladder leading to the hayloft. With one accord they scrambled up. They found that the loft was nearly empty, for a great deal of the hay had been taken to make beds for the American army. Gil sat down on the bare floor, blew on his fingers to warm them, and unfastened the red kerchief in which Jenifer had wrapped the food. Squatting

Trapping a Spy

beside him, Danny reached hungrily for some bread and cheese.

The boys talked softly together as they ate, planning just what they should say when they were stopped by the sentry on the outskirts of Philadelphia, and how they would gain an entrance into the Emmets' house on Chestnut Street.

"Ezra will have locked things up tight," Gil said, biting into a doughnut, "but I know a way to get in through——"

He stopped suddenly, for Danny was making violent motions for him to be quiet. Beneath them the barn door was slowly creaking open. Someone had come in and seemed to be standing directly under them. Danny spied a long crack in the floor near his feet, leaned over, and peeked through. When he lifted his face his eyes were puzzled.

"It's Tom Maddock," he whispered softly. "Wonder what he's doing here."

Bending down, Gil looked through the crack too. Even in the dim light of the stable he had no trouble in recognizing Mr. Thomas Maddock's big nose, or the black fur cap which he always wore when he crossed the river and came to the village of

Silver for General Washington

Valley Forge. Apparently Mr. Maddock had an appointment in the stable, for he moved about stealthily as though he expected to find someone hiding in one of the stalls. Then he stationed himself near the door, which he had left slightly open.

He had not long to wait before the door swung wider and another man came in. Danny clutched at Gil's arm, and Gil's heart skipped a beat, for the newcomer was a tall and stooped man who carried a cane in his right hand and wore his gray queue neatly tucked into a snakeskin bag.

Glancing about hastily, the second man took a stand just inside the open door so that he could see anyone who might approach the stable. Evidently he was sure that he and Maddock were alone, for when he spoke, although his voice was low, it was loud enough so that Gil and Danny could overhear what he was saying.

"Have you brought it?" he asked quickly.

Tom Maddock nodded. Removing his fur cap he took a folded paper from the crown. "Here, Mr. Worrell," he said, handing the paper to his companion. "Every man on the list has food hidden away that he'll sell to the King's army."

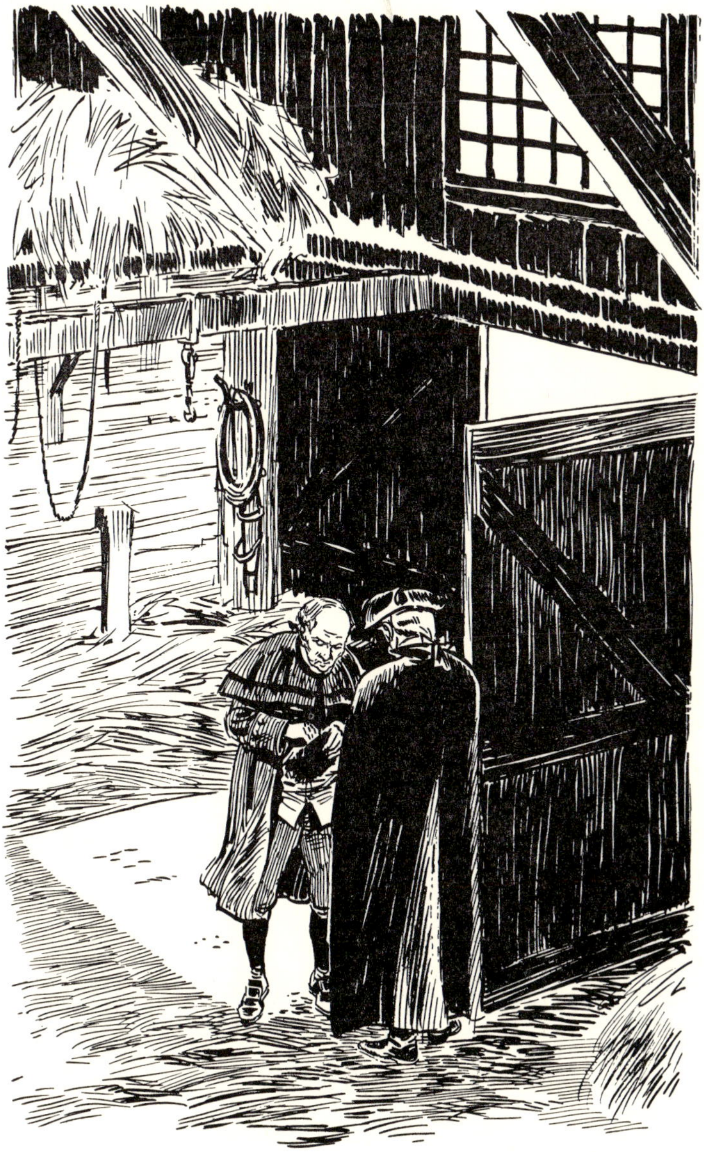

Silver for General Washington

"And the map?" Mr. Worrell asked sharply. "Have you the map?"

"It's there, right under the list," Maddock explained.

Mr. Worrell unfolded the paper and scanned it hastily. "Capital!" he exclaimed softly. "Here's your money—in gold, as we agreed." Into Maddock's outstretched hand he put several coins which he had taken from his purse. "Count them," he commanded.

Eagerly Thomas Maddock counted the coins, clinking one against the other. "That's right," he said. "Just right." He took a little bag from under his coat and slipped the money into it. Muttering something which the boys could not hear very well about "next Thursday," he stepped outside and walked away.

Worrell stuck his head through the door and looked quickly around the yard to be sure that no one was approaching the stable. Then, to the amazement of Danny and Gil, who still had their eyes glued to the crack in the floor of the loft, he picked up his cane, which he had propped against the wall, carefully unscrewed the gold handle and

Trapping a Spy

took it off. Rolling the paper which Maddock had given him into a ball, he slipped it into a cavity near the top of the stick. This done, he screwed the handle on again, and leaning on the cane as though he were lame he stepped out of the stable.

Gil sat up, his eyes blazing. "Sneaking old spies," he exclaimed wrathfully, scrambling to his feet. "Come on. We mustn't let them get away."

Grabbing what remained of the food, he stuffed it into his greatcoat pocket and started down the ladder. Danny slung the bag which contained the chicken over his shoulder and followed him quickly—so quickly that he almost stepped on Gil's fingers, missed a rung in the ladder, and fell to the bottom carrying the other boy along with him. By the time he and Gil had picked themselves up and opened the barn door, Mr. Thomas Maddock was nowhere in sight. But the man with his queue in a snakeskin bag had crossed the yard and was just entering the inn.

The boys held a whispered consultation.

"No use trying to chase Maddock," Danny said, rubbing his knee which had been badly bumped. "We can get Mr. Worrell, though."

Silver for General Washington

Gil nodded. "I'll go in the front way and you go to the back. If he tries to slip out before you can get anybody to help you, yell 'spy' and hang on until someone comes."

"All right!" Danny agreed, and started off toward the kitchen.

Gil crossed the yard and went into the inn. The tavern hall was dark. To the left, two doors were shut tightly, but the door to the taproom on the right was open wide and from it came the sounds of men's voices. Cautiously Gil flattened himself against the wall and peered in.

Three shabbily dressed American officers stood with their backs to him before the big fireplace at the opposite end of the room, evidently waiting for breakfast. At a table to one side of the room, Worrell was just sitting down in a chair which faced the door. There was no one else about.

Taking great care not to be seen, Gil watched Worrell put his hat on the table and then lay his cane carefully on the floor between the wall and himself. Until this minute the boy had had no clear idea of how he could trap the spy. But the instant Worrell laid the cane down Gil made a plan. To his delight, Worrell, having settled himself comfortably, now took a letter from his pocket and began to read it. This gave Gil his chance.

Walking quietly into the room as though he intended to speak with one of the soldiers, the boy passed the spy's table and stopped a few feet behind him. Then crouching close to the wall he stole forward. Bending low he reached out for the cane and began to slide it slowly along the floor. Inch by inch he pulled it toward him until he had the heavy stick nearly out from under the table. Then, to his consternation, the gold head caught on the table leg. The stick slipped, turned, and hit against the heel of Worrell's boot.

Jumping as though he had been shot, Worrell reached quickly for his cane. Finding that it was not where he had laid it, he sprang to his feet, knocking his chair over with a clatter, swung around and made a lunge for Gil. But Gil, with the cane in his hand, had run to the soldiers who had turned around to see what was causing the commotion. Worrell came after him with his fist upraised and his face red with anger.

"Give that back, you young rapscallion," he said

Silver for General Washington

threateningly. "Give me back my cane at once."

"No!" Gil stammered, so excited that he could hardly speak. "No, I won't. No."

"Oh, yes, you will!" one of the soldiers exclaimed, grabbing Gil by the collar and pushing him toward Worrell, who now had both hands on his stick and was pulling with all his might. "Come, we want no thieves around here. Give the gentleman back his property."

"No," Gil cried again, clinging desperately to the cane. Then suddenly the words he wanted tumbled from his lips. "He's a spy. Look, the cane opens. There's a paper in it. He's a spy, I tell you! He's a spy. Oh, don't let him get away."

But at the word "paper," Worrell had made a dash for the door. Before anyone could catch him he had loosened the reins of the horse which stood before the tavern and sprung into the saddle. He galloped away like the wind, and by the time one of the officers was able to get another horse from the stable and start out after him, the spy was so far on his way to Philadelphia that there was no hope of catching him.

Unscrewing the top of the cane which Gil had

Trapping a Spy

thrust into his hands, one of the American officers removed the paper, and smoothed it out carefully. On it was a list of names of seven men living in or near Valley Forge, who Maddock had said were willing to help the British cause. And under the list there was a well-drawn map of the village and of the surrounding country, with the homes of these men so plainly marked that any spy or scout from the British army who sought information or supplies would know just where to go.

By the time the officer had read the list the taproom was in a turmoil. Attracted by the noise and the cry of "spy," the innkeeper, the servants, and the guests had flocked into the room, all demanding at once to be told who the spy was, and where he had gone, and what he had been doing. Gil and Danny, who had come in through the kitchen, quickly found themselves surrounded by a noisy crowd. Again and again in answer to many questions they described Thomas Maddock and Mr. Worrell. Again and again, while the officers examined the map, the two boys were forced to repeat the conversation they had overheard in the barn. At last Gil nudged Danny's elbow.

"We'd better be on our way," he whispered, "else the soldiers will make us go back to camp to tell this all over again, and we'll never get to Philadelphia."

Danny nodded. Watching his chance he began to edge his way slowly toward the door. It was just at that moment that a wagoner who was standing near a window at one side of the fireplace gave a whoop of excitement.

"There's that traitor, Tom Maddock—a-sneakin' 'round the springhouse," he yelled. "Get out of my way." And nearly knocking over two men who stood in front of him he rushed out of the inn by way of the kitchen. Several other people pushed after him and in the confusion which followed Danny and Gil made their escape.

The boys did not follow the road as they ran from the inn, but ducked into the woods. Stumbling over branches and pushing through the underbrush they kept going for nearly a mile. Then Gil sat down on a fallen oak tree and rubbed his leg.

"I wish Mr. Worrell hadn't got clear away," he mourned. "He wouldn't have if I hadn't let that dratted cane slip."

Trapping a Spy

Danny grinned. "Well, you got the map and the list," he said comfortingly. "And Mr. Worrell will never dare show his face in Valley Forge again."

"What will they do to Tom Maddock?" Gil asked.

"Give him two hundred lashes on his bare back for selling information to the enemy, maybe," Danny replied soberly. "That will likely near kill him. Or else they'll hang him the way they hanged that spy they caught last month. I wouldn't want to be in his boots."

"Nor would I," Gil declared gravely.

They talked about the spies until they were rested enough to go on. Leaving the woods they set out again on the road which led toward the city. The day was gray and bleak but they plodded steadily ahead, stopping at midday at a farmhouse to beg for a drink of water. Fortunately, the woman who answered their knock was a kindly Quakeress, who insisted that they warm themselves by her fire and share some hot soup which she was setting out for her children. Then her husband, who had an errand in Radnor, gave the boys a ride that far in his two-wheeled cart.

Silver for General Washington

Yet in spite of this good luck, late afternoon found Gil and Danny still a good eight miles from Philadelphia and too tired to go on much farther. Indeed, Gil was just about to suggest that they begin to look about for a barn or shed where they could spend the night, when a wagon which had been coming along behind them, passed them and stopped.

As the boys drew abreast of it the driver, a friendly-looking old man with shaggy gray hair and a wart on his chin, leaned down and spoke to them.

"Goin' far?" he asked.

"A fair distance," Gil replied.

"Then climb up and ride," the man suggested. "I crave someone to talk to."

He reached down a hand and helped first Gil and then Danny over the wheel. Flapping his reins he clucked to his horse and the wagon started forward.

"My name's McGraw and I'm takin' this wood to the Walnut Street jail in Philadelphia," the man announced, shifting over on his seat to make more room for the boys. "No doubt you're thinkin', if you're smart lads at all, that that's a long way to be haulin' wood. And you're right. But you see——"

He looked down soberly at the boys. "You see, I've got a son in that prison. Andy McGraw, his name is, an' he was captured by the redcoats after he fought them at Germantown. He'd near to dyin' in that jail, he an' all his friends; what with their wounds and the cold and havin' nothin' to eat. And there's naught that I can do about it, save to take wood there and hope that they'll get some of it to warm themselves by, and sometimes to bribe the guard to slip them some morsels of food."

"Have you food for them today?" Gil asked.

"Only a wee bit," the old man replied. "The redcoats have raided our farm again and again and have taken almost all we have."

"That's a sorry state of things," Gil declared.

Danny looked up in alarm, for he was afraid that his cousin was going to give away the two doughnuts and the bit of meat which they had saved for supper. But Gil had other things in mind.

He knew that the old Walnut Street jail which Mr. McGraw had mentioned was not very far from his father's house on Chestnut Street. If only Mr. McGraw could get himself and Danny past the sen-

Silver for General Washington

try on the outskirts of the city and carry them as far as the jail, they would be almost at the end of their journey.

In return for this they would give him the hen in Danny's sack and perhaps he could get the hen to his son. In this way old Speckle would make a meal for American soldiers instead of a meal for redcoats. And Danny and he would get to the Emmet house that night.

This scheme seemed such a good one that Gil told the others about it at once. At the same time he explained to Mr. McGraw why he and Danny were going to Philadelphia.

The old man listened carefully. "It's a fine brave thing you plan to do," he declared when Gil had finished. "I'll help you all I am able. Snow will be fallin', likely, by the time we get to Middle Ferry at the Schuylkill, where the guard stands. It will be near dark too. Both of you crouch 'way back under the seat just before we reach there, and I'll warrant I can get you by without a speck of trouble."

So it happened that two hours later, in the midst of a driving snowstorm, Mr. McGraw drew up his

Trapping a Spy

wagon at the corner of Walnut and Sixth streets and waited before he turned into the prison yard, while the boys thanked him hastily for his help and climbed down over the wheel.

"Stick close so you won't get lost," Gil told Danny, and set off, half-walking, half-running, for he was anxious to reach the Emmet home before it grew so dark that he could not find a way to get into the house.

Danny, who was excited at the thought of being in enemy territory and in a big city too, was eager for a chance to look around. But the snow was almost blinding and it was all he could do to keep up with Gil. Because of the storm few people were abroad. Through the candle-lit windows of a coffee shop the boys caught sight of a group of redcoats, eating and talking. In the doorways of several houses where British officers were quartered, sentinels stood on guard. It seemed to Gil that otherwise the city was little changed. Hurrying along with his teeth chattering and his feet nearly frozen, he spoke to Danny.

"We'll build a good hot fire in the kitchen fireplace as soon as we get inside," he told him. "Maybe we can find some food which Martha forgot to take along when she and Ezra went to New Jersey."

Catching Danny's arm, he steered him into Chestnut Street, almost knocking over the lamplighter who was lighting the lamp at the corner. The man called after the boys angrily, and Gil shouted back an apology. But he did not slacken his pace.

"We're almost home now," he said. "It's there,

Trapping a Spy

right across the——" He stopped abruptly and stood still, staring with open mouth at the house across the way. Danny heard him draw in his breath sharply. "Why, it's lighted!" he gasped. "Our house—it's all lighted up. There are lights in my father's study. Don't you see?"

Danny nodded. Lights did indeed gleam from the lower windows of the house just across the street. At that very moment a British soldier appeared at the window and drew the curtains shut. Then the front door was pulled open. Two young men stepped out, hesitating in the doorway while they buttoned greatcoats over uniforms of scarlet and gold. Talking and laughing together they came down the steps and walked off arm in arm.

Gil stood looking after them, speechless with surprise and dismay.

"Well," Danny announced, beating his arms against his body, "this is a pretty kettle of fish. What shall we do now, Gil? Where shall we go?"

Gil shook his head. "I don't know," he confessed miserably. "I just don't know."

CHAPTER TWELVE

Ezra Is Frightened

For one dreadful minute Gil stood staring at the house. He was furious at the thought that the British were occupying his home. And he had not the faintest idea what he and Danny should do next, nor where they could go to spend the night. Of course, they might try to find one of his father's friends who would help them. But he did not know which of these friends were still in the city and which had fled before the arrival of the enemy. However, he was just about to suggest to Danny that they set out in search of some one of them when a better idea occurred to him.

"Give me a leg up over the garden wall," he told Danny. "I want to prowl around a bit and see what's going on in the house. Maybe the stable is open, or the shed behind the kitchen is empty. Then

Ezra Is Frightened

we'll have a place where we can get in out of the storm."

Danny sneezed. "I'll go too," he declared. "Open the gate for me when you get inside."

"All right," Gil agreed. He looked quickly in either direction. "No one is coming. Now's the time," he said.

Together both boys ran across the cobblestone street. Standing close to the garden wall, Danny bent over with his hands on his knees. Gil stepped on his back, clambered to the top of the wall, and dropped lightly into the garden. In no time at all he had opened the gate and Danny was with him again.

A row of bushes grew close to the side of the house. Running across the rose garden, the boys took shelter behind them, lest someone from an upstairs window should see them. To the rear of the house and connected with it by a covered passageway there was a low building which contained the kitchen, the tiny room where Martha and Ezra had lived, and a storeroom where all sorts of odds and ends were kept. From the window of the kitchen a light gleamed through the falling snow. Stooping

Silver for General Washington

behind the bushes, the boys quietly worked their way toward the light and peered in though the window.

The first things Danny saw as he peeked in were a bubbling pot hung over a blazing fire and a roast of beef, a loaf of bread, a mound of butter, and a large pie set out on the table. The first thing Gil saw was a British soldier, standing beside the table, arranging pewter tankards on a tray.

The sight infuriated him. "Those are my father's tankards," he spluttered angrily, forgetting that only a thin pane of glass separated him from the soldier. "That man has no right——" But the rest of the words were choked down his throat as Danny clapped a hand quickly over his mouth.

"He'll hear you, you zany," Danny whispered fiercely, and he pulled the other boy below the level of the window sill.

For some time the two crouched there waiting to see whether or not the soldier would look out. But apparently he had heard nothing, for he did not appear, and when they peeped into the kitchen again he and the tray full of tankards had vanished. Now another man—a Negro—stood at the table,

Ezra Is Frightened

slicing the roast beef with a large knife. At the sight of this man Gil cried out in astonishment.

"Why, that's Ezra!" he exclaimed and he tapped on one of the little window panes. "Ezra, Ezra," he called softly. "Come and let us in."

Frightened nearly out of his wits by the tapping, Ezra dropped his knife with a clatter. His mouth fell open. His eyes grew big and he looked for all the world as though he expected to see a ghost step into the room right over the window sill. But when Gil tapped again the Negro straightened up, moved slowly toward the kitchen door, opened it a crack, and peeped timidly out.

"Who's there?" he whispered in a shaky voice.

"It's me, Ezra—Danny and me," Gil said, stepping out from behind the bushes. "Please let us in. We're near frozen."

Pulling the door open wider, Gil pushed Danny into the warm kitchen and stumbled after him. Still trembling with fear, Ezra closed the door quietly.

"Land sakes, Master Gillbert, why did you scare me so?" he scolded, staring at Gil. "What you both doin' here anyhow? Don't you know the Britishers have took this house? Don't you know it ain't safe for you to be here?" He looked up sharply. "Sh! Someone is comin' down the passageway," he whispered. "Git yourselves into that storeroom, quick, an' don't you make a sound."

Shoving the boys into the dark storeroom he closed the door hastily behind them. When the British soldier stepped into the kitchen a moment later with an empty tray in his hands, Ezra was down on his knees wiping the floor and talking loudly to himself.

"Nasty ol' water jes' spilled itself all over my clean floor," Ezra grumbled, trying at the same time to hide the boys' snowy footprints by rubbing them into a puddle.

But the British orderly did not even look his way.

"Step lively, black man," the soldier commanded, reaching for a slice of roast beef and stuffing a piece of it into his mouth. "The Colonel wants his supper and he wants it in a hurry."

Meekly Ezra stood up, put away his cloth, and began to prepare food for the four British officers who had taken up their quarters in his master's house. He clattered dishes together, dropped a big kettle, and made all manner of noise, hoping to

Ezra Is Frightened

cover up any sounds which might come from the storeroom. But behind that closed door everything was very still.

There was just enough light sifting through the narrow high window of the storeroom so that Danny and Gil could see what they were doing. Taking great care not to bump the big chest which was propped against the wall, nor to fall over any of the other furniture, Gil took off his greatcoat and folded it, dry side out, to make a pillow. Sitting down on it, with his back against the chimney, which was warm from the kitchen fire, he began to remove his wet shoes and stockings. Danny followed his example and soon both boys had rubbed life and heat into their cold numb feet.

With one of the enemy so close they hardly dared to whisper, and before long it became so dark that they could not even make signs to one another. Remembering hungrily the roast beef and pie which he had seen on the kitchen table, Danny curled up on the floor and began before long to dream about them. But Gil, with his knees drawn up under his chin, sat staring into the blackness and thinking hard.

Silver for General Washington

How, he wondered, could he and Danny possibly dig up the chest and get the silver for which they had come all the way from Valley Forge when redcoats were living right in the house? And why was Ezra, who was supposed to be in New Jersey with his wife and daughter, now in the next room preparing a meal for the enemy? Over and over he asked himself these two questions, but found no answer to either of them. At last with a sigh he gave up, lay down beside Danny, pulled his greatcoat over both of them, and was soon fast asleep.

When Ezra opened the storeroom door several hours later he found the two boys still slumbering soundly.

"Wake up, Master Gilbert," he whispered, shaking Gil gently. "The Britishers has all gone to their beds an' is sleepin'. I want you an' Master Danny to git some hot food into yourselfs right away an' then to tell me what you both are doin' here."

Rubbing their eyes and yawning, the boys stumbled barefooted into the warm kitchen and sat down before a small table which Ezra had set close to the fire. Danny whistled softly when he saw the food on his plate and Gil grinned with delight.

"Talk low and eat good," Ezra told them. "You both look a lot thinner than when I seen you last in Valley Forge."

Gil nodded. "Everybody's thin there," he said, smearing great chunks of butter on his bread. "Seems as if the redcoats get all the food. If Seth or Davey could see this——" The rest of the sentence

Silver for General Washington

went unfinished, for he had crammed his mouth so full that he could not speak.

From the cupboard Ezra brought two pieces of shoofly pie. Setting them on the table, he began to explain to Gil how it happened that he was not in New Jersey with Martha and his daughter, Sukey.

"Seems like I couldn't rest as long as I knowed your pappy's house an' all his things had no one to watch over them when the redcoats were a-comin'," he said. "So I jes' left Martha an' come right back. Good thing I done it too, 'cause I been able to keep my eye on them pesky Britishers that moved in, an' now I kin look after you, too. What are you both doin' here anyway, Master Gilbert?"

Gil swallowed a large bite of meat and bread. Between mouthfuls he told Ezra why he and Danny had come to Philadelphia and what they hoped to do. When the boy had finished his story, Ezra shook his head doubtfully.

"There ain't no way you kin dig up that chest when the Britishers is in the house," he said firmly. "They'll hear you, sure, and then where'll you be? No, the only thing you kin do is to wait till some night when they all go out, like they do some-

Ezra Is Frightened

times. Till then you'll jes' have to sleep in the storeroom and eat what I kin sneak to you. Now I'll make you up a good bed on the floor, an' don't you dare stir tomorrow mornin' till I tells you the redcoats has had their breakfast an' the coast is clear."

So began the strangest and most exciting five days which Gil or Danny had ever known. Every night they slept on the storeroom floor. Every morning they ate whatever food Ezra was able to get for them. Then, as soon as he had made sure that it was safe for them to emerge from their hiding place, they slipped out of a back door which opened directly into an alley and spent the greater part of the day roaming about the city.

No matter how tired or hungry they became they did not go into the house again until they saw Ezra's signal—a brown jug set in the kitchen window—which meant that he was alone in the kitchen.

Only twice were the boys nearly caught. Once Gil, who was anxious to see what had happened to the house since the British had moved in, stole into the dining room when he thought no one was about, and from there into his father's study. He had expected to find many articles missing and the rooms in great disorder. But there were few changes.

This made him happy, and he was just thinking that all the redcoats were not so bad as those who had wrecked the homes in Valley Forge, when he heard a step on the stairs. Ducking into the closet he waited, trembling, while one of the officers came into the study, took some papers from the desk, and went upstairs again. Then he fled quietly back to the storeroom.

Another time when Danny was in the kitchen, Ezra did not hear the orderly approaching, and the soldier walked in to find the boy warming himself before the fire. But Ezra thought quickly. Pretending that Danny was the butcher's boy he scolded him roundly for being so late with the meat, and shoved him crossly out of the door. Poor Danny had had to wait shivering outside until the orderly had left the kitchen and it was safe for him to return.

Fortunately for the boys the weather was good. There was no more snow and the days were sunny. When Gil and Danny had first arrived in Philadelphia, Gil had thought the city seemed little changed.

Ezra Is Frightened

In the light of day, however, he saw that it was different in many ways.

No longer was it a quiet, slow-moving place where sober Quakers and other citizens went about their business in peace. Now the streets were thronged with men and women. Redcoats and Hessians paraded up and down the cobblestone thoroughfares. Officers clattered through the city on horseback or rode proudly about in carrying chairs and chaises. Stores were well filled. Taverns and coffee shops were gay with laughter and noise. Balls and parties were held frequently and life was very pleasant for those who were loyal to the King.

There were other changes, too, in Philadelphia, which Gil noticed as he and Danny wandered about. No longer could a boy investigate the sailing ships tied at the wharves in the Delaware River, for pickets stood guard over them. Soldiers were camped here and there on the outskirts of the city, and to the north a row of nine strong forts stretched from one river to the other.

As yet neither Gil nor Danny knew how they were going to get out of the city, for they had no pass to show the pickets.

"Maybe we can find a spot along the Schuylkill that is not well guarded and cross on the ice," Danny suggested.

With this thought in mind the boys studied the fortifications carefully and noted where the sentinels were posted. They found that the southern fringes of the city were not so well picketed as the northern. So they decided to follow the road to Gray's Ferry, to turn south along the river until they were opposite Mr. Bartram's famous gardens, to cross the ice, and then to make their way back to the Lancaster Road over which they had traveled in coming to Philadelphia.

To Gil, who was anxious to get back to the encampment with the silver for General Washington, the days seemed endless. Sometimes he thought that the time would never come when Ezra would say it was safe for them to dig up the chest. But one evening after the boys had gone to bed, Ezra appeared at the storeroom door with two shovels, two sacks, and a lantern.

"They is all gone to see the play at the Old South Theater, an' the house is empty," he announced.

Danny gave a whoop of joy, and Gil, hardly

Ezra Is Frightened

daring to believe his ears, asked, "Are you certain?"

Ezra nodded. "Git your clothes on and don't waste no time. Diggin' up that chest ain't goin' to be no easy job."

As quickly as possible the two boys dressed and followed Ezra to the low cellar. Gil brushed cobwebs from his face, and decided that no one had been down there since the night the chest had been buried. He could remember just the spot where it had been placed, for he had at that time noticed a black stain on the beam overhead. Leading the way he took a shovel from Ezra and began to dig. Danny held the lantern and no one said a word, so intent were they all on finishing their task before the British officers returned.

The ground was hard—so hard that at first it seemed impossible to dig in it at all. Fortunately, however, the chest had not been buried very deep. All three took turns with the shovels and after an hour of good hard work the top of the chest was free at last and scraped clean of earth. Gil wiped the perspiration from his forehead and leaned on his shovel.

"There's no sense in trying to take it out of the

Silver for General Washington

ground if we can get the lid up," he said, and he began to dig around at the back of the chest so that the top could be lifted.

Finally after much tugging and grunting and muttering, the two boys and Ezra were able to force back the cover of the big box. Gil sat back on his heels and looked at the contents soberly. There, just as his father had left them, were the big candlesticks, the goblets, the porringers, the pitcher, the sugar box, the coffeepot, and the great heavy platters.

Tears filled his eyes as he lifted these things out, one by one, and he wondered, as he set the box containing the spoons, knives, and silver-handled forks on the ground beside him, where his father was. No word had come from Mr. Emmet since he had left Philadelphia and a great longing to see his father and to hear him speak swept over Gil.

It was Ezra who interrupted his thoughts.

" 'Pears like to me you're takin' a powerful lot on your shoulders, Master Gil—settin' out to give away all your pappy's fine things," he said. "Ain't you feared he'll be awful cross with you about it?"

Gil shook his head. A picture of ragged, hungry

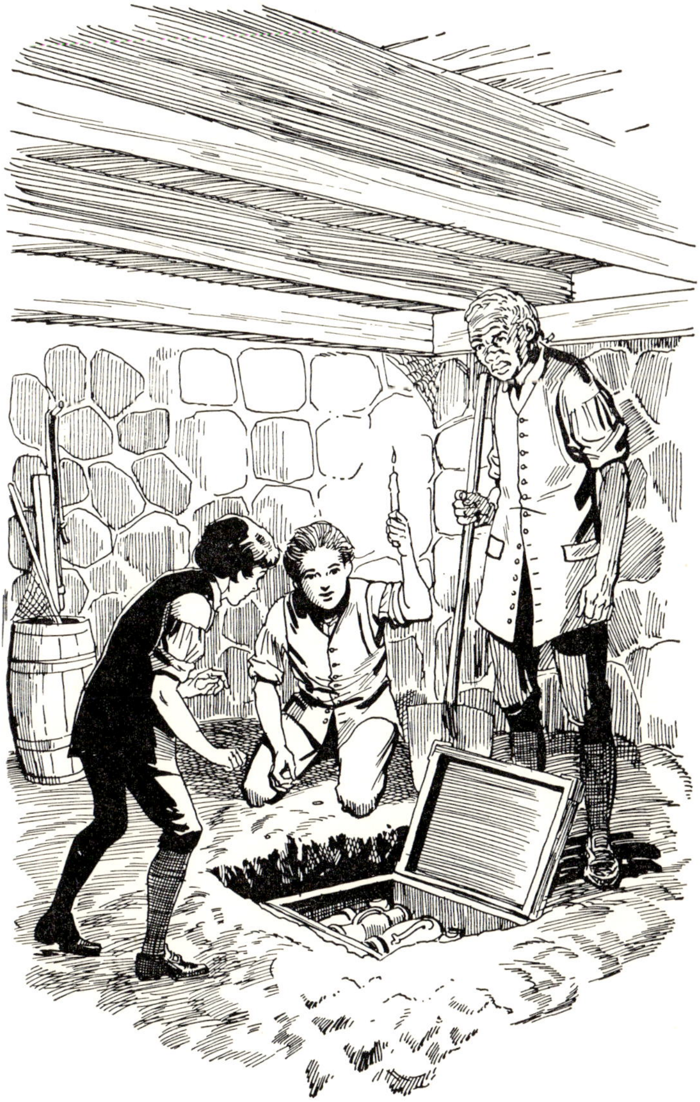

Silver for General Washington

soldiers flashed before his eyes and he could almost hear one of them speaking: "What the General needs to win this war is money—good hard money." He remembered his father's letter.

"No," he declared positively, "my father won't be cross, Ezra. He will say I have done the right thing. I know he will."

Rubbing the mist from his eyes, he began to help Danny put the silver into the two sacks which Ezra had brought for the purpose. It did not take long to shovel the earth over the chest again and to trample the ground down once more. Then, leaving the boys in the cellar, Ezra went upstairs to be sure that none of the redcoats had returned to the house.

Danny lifted one of the sacks.

"I say, that's heavy!" he exclaimed, setting it down quickly again. "How on earth do you think we can get it back to Valley Forge?"

Gil looked worried, and picked up the other sack.

"It is heavy," he confessed. "Lots heavier than I thought it would be. But between us we'll have to manage it somehow."

CHAPTER THIRTEEN

Escape from Philadelphia

STRANGELY enough, it was Ezra who answered the question of how to get the silver to Valley Forge.

"You ain't goin' to take it there at all," he declared when he and the two boys were safely back in the storeroom with the bags of silver at their feet. "It's so big and heavy you'd never git anywhere with it—an' anyhow, I've been thinkin', what would General Washington do with a lot of silver? You done said yourself, Master Gilbert, that what he needs is money."

"He could have it melted down into money," Gil protested.

"But don't you see you ain't never goin' to be able to git it there?" Ezra argued. "Now, look here, Master Gil, I knows there must be someone in this city who is fixed to buy silver like this. Tomorrow is market day an' when I go down to git the food I'll jes' ask around careful-like, an' see if we can't sell it so's you kin take the money back with you. Won't that be better than tryin' to lug these here heavy things clear to Valley Forge?"

"Yes," Gil admitted slowly, wishing he had thought of the scheme himself. "It would be better. It's a good plan, Ezra."

Ezra smiled. "Looks as if I got somethin' 'sides sawdust in this old black head after all," he said and he gave a low chuckle as he went into the kitchen, leaving the two tired boys to fall into bed.

It was not until after dinner the next day that Ezra was free to slip into the storeroom with news of his trip to market. The boys had stayed in their hideout all the morning waiting impatiently for him and they were eager to hear what he had to report. He was in fine spirits, but he was also in a hurry, for it was at an hour of the day when the British orderly was often in and out of the kitchen.

"Don't fret me now with askin' how I foun' this out, 'cause I ain't got time to tell you," he told the boys. "Jes' promise me quick, Master Gil, that you'll not ever speak a word of what I says 'cept maybe to General Washington or to your pappy."

"I vow I won't," Gil declared solemnly.

"So do I," promised Danny.

"Then listen good with all your ears, 'cause I've got everythin' all fixed fer you. Kin you remember, Master Gil, where the Bag of Nails Inn sets on Front Street?"

Gil nodded.

"Next to it is a big house," Ezra went on, "an' right next to that is a little bitty house. When you git to the little house look sharp to see that no one is watchin' you. Then go down the alley to the back door. Knock real quick, four raps, an' then real slow, two raps. Soon as you done this three times someone will come and ask you 'Give the countersign?' an' then you says——" He stopped and scratched his head thoughtfully. "I disremember what you says," he confessed in alarm. "It's the name of some grand French gentleman who has come over here to help us fight the redcoats—Laffy —Laffy——"

"I know—Lafayette!" Gil exclaimed. "He's the French general who has been in Valley Forge."

"That's right," Ezra agreed delightedly, peering

Silver for General Washington

out into the kitchen and listening to hear if anyone were coming. "Well, after you says this Laffyette name you will get let in. Then you give the man your silver an' he will sell it for you an' git you the money."

Danny looked doubtful. "How do you know this man will give Gil the money?" he asked. "Maybe he's a thief and he'll take the silver and keep it."

Ezra shook his head. "No such thing, Master Danny," he said positively. "He is an honest man. I forgot to tell you he knows Master Gil's pappy an' he's workin' in secret against the pesky Britishers, jes' like everybody else who wants to be free." He turned to Gil. "He knows all about you, Master Gil, an' if you does jes' like I tell you you'll be all right," he told him. "Only 'fore you go we'd better cover that silver with some ol' rags, lessen somebody peeps into your sacks. I'll get 'em now."

He left the room and returned shortly with a great bundle of rags. These the boys put around and over the silver, arranging the candlesticks and other pieces in such a way that no one looking at the bags would guess what they contained. Then, putting on

Escape from Philadelphia

their greatcoats, they hoisted the sacks to their shoulders.

"I do pray you git there safe," Ezra said as he pulled open the back door. "Don't you let no one on the street 'spect how heavy them sacks are, or they're like to stop you an' ask you what you're fetchin' and where."

This was easy advice to give, but not so easy to follow, for both Gil and Danny found it difficult not to bend over under the weight of the silver. But they stood as straight as they could and set out bravely.

Chestnut Street was thronged with people. The boys ducked and dodged among the crowd, trying hard not to bump their unwieldy burdens against any of the passers-by. At Second Street they were stopped by a parade of Hessian soldiers.

Afraid to put their sacks down for fear they would never get them on their backs again without attracting attention, Danny and Gil waited impatiently for the green-coated Germans to pass. Gil looked enviously at their smart, warm uniforms, thinking of the ragged soldiers at Valley Forge. And Danny studied the faces under the shining

Silver for General Washington

brass helmets, wondering if the three men who had forced their way into his home, and stolen Gil's violin, were among the stiff-legged marchers. But he did not see them.

As soon as the parade had passed, the boys continued on their way. At each step the sacks seemed to grow heavier, but they reached the Bag of Nails Inn at last and found the little house they were seeking. Looking about first to see that no one was watching them, Gil led the way down the ally and knocked on the back door.

Almost immediately the door was opened just a crack and a low voice said, "The countersign. Quick, give the countersign."

"Lafayette," Danny and Gil whispered together, their hearts pounding with excitement.

At once the door was opened wide enough so that the boys could step inside, and then shut quickly behind them. Gil and Danny found themselves in a narrow, dark hallway. A tall old man with his white wig slightly askew and a candle in his hand stood before them. Holding the candle close to the boys' faces he peered from one to the other with sharp, bright eyes.

Then, apparently satisfied with what he had seen, he motioned to the boys to follow him and led the way down a short flight of stairs to a small cellar room. Except for a table, a high-backed bench, and two chairs, the room was empty. The old man set his candle on the table.

"Put your sacks on the floor," he said, "and then rest yourselves on that bench by the fire. You must be tired."

Still too excited to speak, the boys lowered their

heavy bags carefully to the floor and sat down on the bench. The old man pulled a chair up close to them, seated himself, and tapped Gil on the knee.

"You are Gilbert Emmet's son, are you not?" he asked.

Gil swallowed hard. "Yes, sir," he replied, "and this is my cousin, Danny Gardner, who lives in Valley Forge."

The old man smiled. "You look like your father, young Emmet!" he said. "He came here many times before he left the city and I went often to your house when we were first laying our plans to fight for independence. But you were always busy at your lessons or at play. You do not even know my name, do you?"

"No, sir," Gil said apologetically. "I don't."

"Good," the old man exclaimed. "I'll not tell it to you, either. As long as the enemy is in our city we who are working together for freedom must do all of our work in secret, and the less known about us the better. Now tell me as quickly as you can just what you want me to do for you and why."

Speaking haltingly, Gil began to describe how the soldiers were suffering in Valley Forge and

Escape from Philadelphia

what he wanted to do to help them. Danny interrupted now and then with details and before long the whole story of the boys' trip to Philadelphia and of the unearthing of the silver had been told.

"And so," Gil finished, "when we found it was too heavy to carry, Ezra said we must come to you and that you would help us sell it."

The old man nodded. "I think I can dispose of the silver," he said slowly. "And I have no doubt that your father would want me to do so. I will try to get the money for it in gold, which will be easy for you to carry, but——" He hesitated and a troubled frown wrinkled his forehead. "But unfortunately I know of no way that I can help you get it safely back to Valley Forge. Have you a pass so that you can get by the sentries?"

"No, sir," Gil replied, leaning over to pick up his hat which had dropped to the floor. "We thought we would start very early in the morning and cross the ice over the Schuylkill just below Gray's Ferry. There aren't so many pickets around there, sir, we've heard. We think we can slip past them if we are careful."

The old man scowled uneasily. "I mistrust that

plan," he declared, hitching his chair closer and leaning forward. "It would be less dangerous for you if you could leave late in the afternoon and cross the river after dark. On the right-hand side of the road which leads to Darby, about half a mile south of Gray's Ferry, there is a house where a Mr. Edwards and his family live. They are loyal patriots. If you can get across the river safely and go there, I feel sure that they will give you shelter for the night and help you get on to Valley Forge the next day."

He glanced soberly from one boy to the other. "You both understand, don't you, that you will be in real peril until you are well past the sentries? If either of you is captured it will go hard with you."

"We'll get over the river safely, sir," Gil declared, trying to sound much more courageous than he felt. "Danny can run like a deer and I can very near keep pace with him."

The old man smiled. "Splendid!" he exclaimed. "But remember even when you are running to keep your eyes sharp and your ears keen. Danger lurks in strange places these days."

He rose to his feet and the boys rose with him.

Escape from Philadelphia

"You must go now, for I expect other callers very soon," he said, picking up his candle. "I will sell your silver as quickly as possible, young Emmet. Before the week is out a chimney sweep will come to the back door of your father's house, pretending to ask for work. He will slip Ezra a package which will contain your money. Try to leave the city that same afternoon if you can. When you get to Mr. Edwards' house, knock as you knocked here today. If you are asked for a countersign repeat the word 'Lafayette.' Is that all clear?"

"Yes, sir," Gil replied, and Danny nodded slowly.

"Good!" exclaimed the old man, starting up the stairs. "There is only one thing more. After you have given your money to General Washington, please give him this message for me. Tell him that there are still many people in Philadelphia who are working for him and his army in every way that they can, despite the enemy now living in the city. Tell him also that we look to him to lead us to victory and that we know he will not fail us."

He stopped, for they had reached the door, and shook hands gravely with each boy.

Silver for General Washington

"You are brave lads and true patriots," he said. "God grant you a safe journey back to Valley Forge." Then, opening the door, he made sure that no one was about who would see the boys leave the house, and quickly let them out.

Gil and Danny hurried to the Emmet home at once to tell Ezra what had happened and to wait impatiently for the chimney sweep to bring the money. They hardly dared to leave the house for the next few days, lest he come while they were out. And they were in the storeroom reading over some old copies of *Poor Richard's Almanac* when he arrived late one afternoon.

Pounding on the kitchen door, the sweep announced in a loud voice that he had been told to come to clean the chimneys. In an equally loud voice Ezra replied that someone must have made a mistake—that the chimneys did not need cleaning, and that when they did he would get the regular sweep to attend to them. During this conversation a packet which the sweep had brought hidden in his wooden bucket was passed quickly from one man to the other.

As soon as the sweep had left, Ezra took this

Escape from Philadelphia

packet to the storeroom. With eager hands Gil unfastened it and took from it two linen money belts, stiff and heavy with the coins which had been stitched in them.

"There must be enough money here to feed a hundred men for months!" Danny gasped as he lifted the belts.

Gil nodded excitedly as he unbuttoned his jacket, pulled up his shirt and wrapped one of the strips around his waist. "This is a fine way to carry it," he whispered. "Put yours on, Danny, and let's get on our way at once."

"You ain't goin' to go till I git you some food to take with you," Ezra said, and went to the kitchen to wrap up something for the boys to eat along the way.

Danny put his belt on and buttoned his jacket over it with difficulty.

"It feels like a board," he declared, wriggling around inside his clothes, "and my jacket fits so snug I can scarce breathe."

"Loosen it, then. Leave it open," Gil advised him. He reached for his greatcoat. "I wish Ezra would hurry!" he exclaimed impatiently. "If we

Silver for General Washington

start right away we can just get to Gray's Ferry before it is too dark to see where we're going."

"It won't get that dark tonight," Danny reminded him wryly, unbuttoning his jacket. "There will be a moon. A big bright moon, Gil, that will show us up in a pretty fashion when we cross the river. Maybe——" he hesitated. "Maybe we'd better wait until a darker night. When I think about those sentries and their guns I get a terrible mixed-up feeling in my stomach."

Gil grinned. "You're scared," he said softly. "So am I." Then, speaking as much to encourage himself as Danny, he added, "Everybody's afraid sometimes, I think—even General Washington. My father told me that the only really brave men are the ones who are afraid and who go right ahead anyway. So pull on your greatcoat and let's start."

Danny nodded and stuck his arms into the sleeves of his coat. By the time he had buttoned it Ezra had returned with a packet of food for each boy.

Little time was spent in saying good-by and ten minutes later Gil and Danny were well on their way up Chestnut Street. The sun was low in the sky. Although the day had been warm for Febru-

Escape from Philadelphia

ary, a cold wind was blowing, and no one paid any attention to the two boys who hurried along toward the southern edge of the city, with their collars turned up around their ears and their hands plunged deep into their pockets. Soon they had left the center of the city behind and were out on the country road which led to Gray's Ferry.

The sun had set when they turned off this road and struck out to the left, down a lane which led past farms, fields, and patches of woodland, to a spot some distance below the ferry, where they believed no pickets had been stationed. A farmer carrying buckets of milk from his barn to his house looked after the boys curiously when they passed, but no one else seemed to be about.

By the time Gil and Danny had reached the river the first stars were out and the tip of the moon was just showing through the trees. Crouching low behind some bushes which grew not far from the river's edge, the boys waited tensely. Their ears were sharp to catch the sound of a picket's step. Their eyes were keen to make out the figure of any soldier who might be guarding the shore. But they heard nothing except the pounding of their own

Silver for General Washington

hearts. And they saw nothing save the shadowy trees, a few patches of snow, and the ice on the river, now gleaming faintly in the ever increasing moonlight.

"It's melting," Danny whispered, staring at the ice. "Do you think it will hold us?"

"We'd better test it along the edges before we cross," Gil said. And dropping to his hands and knees he crept slowly and carefully toward the river with Danny just behind him. At the river's edge both boys straightened up. And at that very instant a soldier stepped out from behind the trunk of a large oak tree—a huge man with a musket.

"Halt," he cried sharply. "Who goes there?"

Speechless with fright Gil and Danny stood motionless. But only for a second.

"Run for it," Gil whispered fiercely, and both boys sped out over the ice, which cracked with a loud snapping noise and gave ominously under their feet but did not break.

"Halt!" the sentry shouted again. "Halt, or I'll fire!"

"Run," Gil panted, not realizing that Danny was already far ahead of him. "Run! Keep going!"

Escape from Philadelphia

A musket shot cracked through the still night air, and a bullet whizzed. Gil felt a stab of pain above his left knee. Stumbling in the half-frozen slush, he regained his footing and went on again, slowly now and limping badly. He could hear men's voices shouting behind him. Glancing over his shoulder he saw that the sentry was sprinting after him. Another soldier stood on the shore.

"Keep going," Gil told himself, clapping his hand over the wound in his leg.

Suddenly the ice made a roaring noise and crackled sharply. There was a cry of terror behind him as the heavy sentry crashed through into the water. Thrashing about wildly he shouted for help. The other soldier ran to his assistance and Gil reached the opposite shore in safety. Grabbing the hand which Danny held out to him he climbed painfully up the bank.

"That was a close shave," Danny whispered when the two boys had gained the shelter of a thick clump of laurel bushes. "It's lucky for us he was such a poor shot."

"He wasn't," Gil told him with a shaky grin. "He nicked me in the leg."

Silver for General Washington

Danny drew in his breath sharply.

"Is it bad?" he asked, bending over to peer at a spot above Gil's knee where the blood was oozing through his breeches. "Can you make the Edwards' house?"

"I think I can walk, but I can't go fast enough," Gil gasped, leaning on him heavily. "There may be other soldiers coming." He fumbled at the buttons of his greatcoat. "Help me get this thing off," he demanded, reaching inside his jacket and yanking at the money belt around his waist. Pulling it free he thrust it at Danny. "Take it," he said quickly. "Get it to Mr. Edwards' house. I'll come after you as fast as I can."

Danny shook his head violently. "I'll never leave you here alone," he declared. "Never!"

Gil wailed despairingly. "Go, please go," he begged. "I can manage somehow even if they capture me but if they take the money that we got for General Washington and the men at Valley Forge——"

"They won't," Danny promised shortly. "I'll go and be back as soon as I can, to help you." And he set off, dodging behind trees and bushes, in the

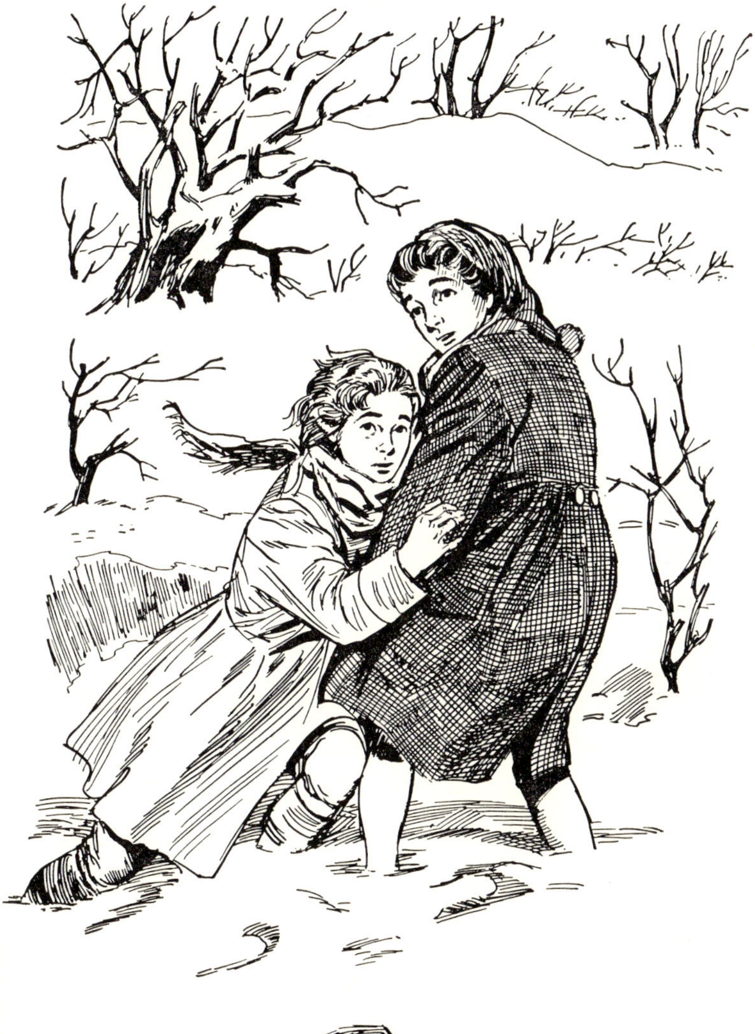

direction of the road which led toward Darby.

Gil watched him for a moment. Then he looked toward the river where, with the help of the soldier who had come to his rescue, the sentry was just climbing out of the icy water. The boy expected that at any minute other soldiers stationed on the west bank of the Schuylkill above the ferry might come on the run to see what had caused the musket shot and what the shouting had been about. He was determined to get as far from the river's edge as possible before this happened.

Unfastening the buckle at his knee, he shoved up the leg of his breeches and looked at his wound. It was bleeding freely.

"That bullet took a good big piece out of me," he muttered rather proudly.

Taking his handkerchief from his pocket, he wrapped it around his leg and tied it tightly. Then gritting his teeth he tried to walk. Shivers of pain ran up and down his leg. Perspiration broke out on his forehead. He felt weak and rather sick. But he found, even so, that he could get over the ground. Hobbling slowly toward the road he set out in the direction Danny had taken.

CHAPTER FOURTEEN

Valley Forge Again

It was unusually warm for March in Valley Forge. Melting snows had turned the road which led to General Washington's headquarters into a river of mud. Jenifer picked her way carefully, trying to avoid the worst of the puddles. With one hand she held up her skirts as best she could. In the other she carried a bag containing Aunt Abigail's needles, thimble, scissors, and thread. How Aunt Abigail had happened to forget this bag Jen did not know. Perhaps it was because she was so excited about being invited by Mrs. Washington to sew with the other ladies at headquarters.

Jolly little Mrs. Washington had come by coach to Valley Forge on the day before her husband's birthday, to spend a few months with him. Alarmed by the hunger and sickness she had found among

Silver for General Washington

the soldiers, she had set about at once doing everything she could for them—taking baskets of food and medicine to those who were ill, stopping to chat encouragingly with those who were well, and making warm clothing for as many as possible. Scarcely a day passed that she did not invite some of the officers' wives who lived in the encampment, or a number of women from the village or from nearby farms, to come to her little second-story room in the General's headquarters to sew with her.

Aunt Abigail's invitation had been brought to the Gardner home that morning. Greatly pleased, Aunt Abigail had put on her best gray homespun dress and her finest ruffled fichu, taken the shirts for the soldiers which she had cut from two old linen bed sheets, and set out on the long walk to headquarters, leaving her sewing bag behind her.

"She'll not be able to do a thing without it," Jenifer told herself as she stepped off the road to wait impatiently for a body of troopers to ride by. "Not a thing."

It was a beautiful afternoon. The wind was driving white clouds across a bright blue sky. The air smelled fresh and sweet, and spring seemed to be

Valley Forge Again

just around the next bend in the road. But the lovely weather meant nothing to Jenifer, for she was so worried about Gil and Danny that she could think of little else. She would not soon forget the day they had left. Until nightfall, true to her promise to Gil, she had tried to keep Aunt Abigail and Uncle Benjamin from finding out where the boys had gone and why. At last, worn out by their questioning, she had confessed to them all that she knew about the trip to Philadelphia.

Uncle Benjamin had set out after Gil and Danny on horseback, hoping to overtake them before they tried to enter the city. But he had returned the next day at noon to say that he had found no trace of them except at the King of Prussia Inn. There the innkeeper had described how two boys had caught Thomas Maddock selling information to an enemy spy, how they had managed to get hold of the spy's cane in which the information was hidden, and how they had disappeared while Maddock was being captured.

"He said he thought one of the boys was our Danny," Uncle Benjamin had reported proudly. "The other must have been Gil. If the lads are as

Silver for General Washington

smart as that, I'll not fret too much about them. Nor should you. It's a fine thing they have set out to do and they'll find their way back home in good time."

But the boys had been gone for many days and both Jenifer and Aunt Abigail were sure that something dreadful had happened to them. Jen was thinking of them as she came within sight of the neat sandstone house which General Washington had rented for his winter headquarters. She was close enough to the building to see the thirteen white stars in the General's blue flag as it tossed in the wind, and to make out the faces of a number of women who were hurrying through the gate and into the house. Aunt Abigail was not among them.

"She has gone in already," Jenifer thought, and hastened her steps, hoping that the sentry would let her pass, so that she herself might take Aunt Abigail's sewing things to her.

Walking past the horses which were tied to the hitching posts near the gate, she turned up the path. Much to her surprise the sentry only nodded and said, "Indeed you may, Missy," when she asked if she might knock at the door. And the Negro manservant who answered her knock told her that she

Valley Forge Again

might take the sewing bag right up to Mrs. Washington's sitting room herself.

Excited at being in the house where the Commander in Chief of the American army was living, Jenifer darted quick glances here and there before she started up the stairs, hoping to catch sight of the General or of some of his aides. But there was no one about.

Guided by the soft murmur of voices, she turned down the hall and stopped on the threshold of Mrs. Washington's sitting room. At least a dozen women had gathered there. All were sewing or patching or darning or knitting except Aunt Abigial, who was ripping the basting threads from a coat which someone had made from an old blanket. No one saw Jen and she stood for several minutes not knowing what she should do next. At last Mrs. Washington herself spied her and beckoned to her to come in. Timidly Jenifer crossed the room, dropped a curtsey to the General's wife, and explained why she was there.

"Faith, child! It is a good thing you came," Mrs. Washington exclaimed. "We can always use another pair of hands, and you may pull the bastings from that coat while your aunt sews up the shirts."

Silver for General Washington

Pleased that she was to be allowed to stay, Jen gave Aunt Abigail her sewing bag and began to pull bastings. The ladies looked at her curiously and then went on with their talk.

Most of them talked about the camp and the soldiers and the shortage of food. One woman mentioned the three new markets which had been opened in different places in the encampment, where any soldiers who had money to spend could buy whatever food the farmers had to sell. Another spoke of the bridge which General Sullivan and his New Hampshire men had just built over the Schuylkill so that farmers from the other side of the river would have less trouble in getting their supplies to Valley Forge.

Someone else told of seeing forty-five cows which General Anthony Wayne's foragers had rounded up in New Jersey and driven to the camp. They were very thin because they had walked so far, she said, but even so she had heard that the soldiers had had meat for dinner for three days. At this, a woman who was knitting on the longest stocking Jenifer had ever seen, spoke her mind about several farmers across the river who were

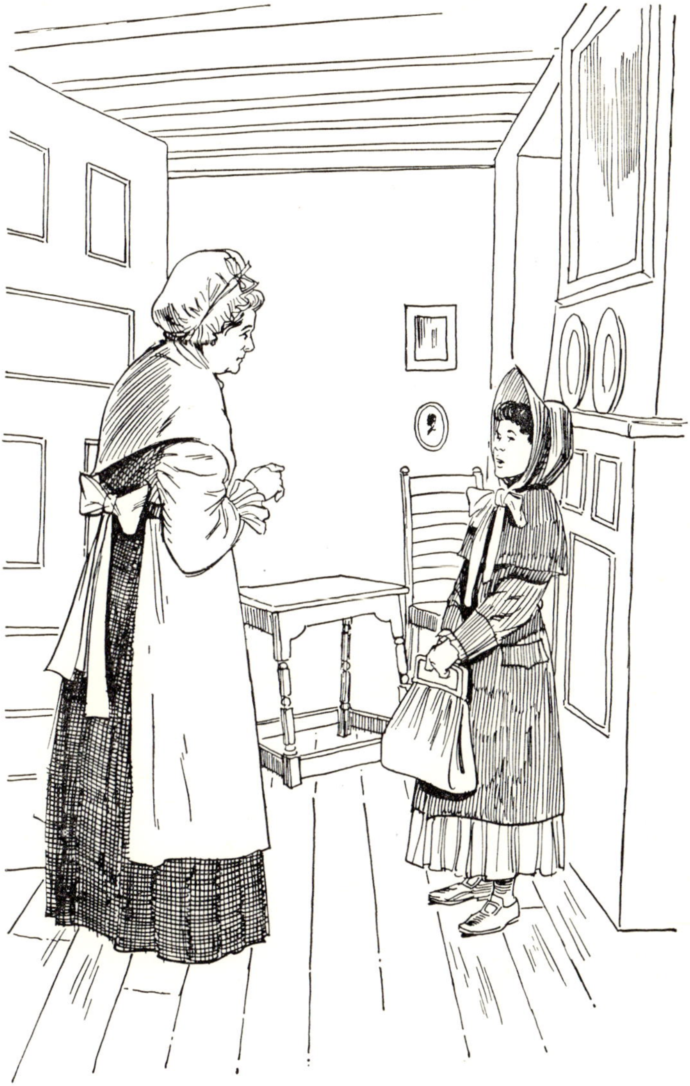

Silver for General Washington

suspected of selling food and cattle to the enemy.

This, in turn, led to a discussion of the traitor —Thomas Maddock—who was now in prison waiting to be tried. And Mrs. Gardner was just about to announce that her son and her nephew had helped to capture Maddock, when a servant appeared in the doorway with a tray on which was a tiny piece of johnnycake and a cup of loosestrife tea for every lady. Then suddenly the afternoon was over and Jenifer found herself walking with Aunt Abigail toward home.

For some time the two talked together about the General's wife, remarking on how kind and friendly she was, and smiling over the way she called her dignified husband "my old man." Then Jenifer blurted out the question which was always in her mind.

"Aunt Abigail, how can we find Danny and Gil?"

Usually Aunt Abigail answered this question with a sad shake of her head. This time she replied decidedly, "If those boys haven't returned by tomorrow night, I shall beg Mrs. Washington to ask the General to help us find them."

Valley Forge Again

But it was not necessary to go to Mrs. Washington for help in finding the boys. For the very next evening just as the Gardners were sitting down to supper there came a great pounding at the front door. Uncle Benjamin went to see who was there. A moment later his voice rang out joyfully.

"Abby! Abby!" he shouted. "It's Gil and our Danny. I told you they'd get back safe."

Dropping the bread which she was carrying, Aunt Abigail flew to the door. Jen, Patsy, and Evan crowded after her down the narrow hall. And there standing on the step were Gil and Danny, and rumbling off down the road in the direction of the camp was the big wagon in which they had arrived.

It had been raining all the afternoon; the boys were wet, cold, hungry, and almost too tired to speak. Jenifer cried out in distress when she saw that Gil was leaning heavily on a homemade crutch.

But he hobbled into the kitchen, telling her with pride, "It's nothing, Jen. A bullet nicked me—that's all. It will be well soon."

Nevertheless, he was glad to sit down on the chair which Aunt Abigail pushed close to the fire, and to prop his leg up on the footstool which Patsy

Silver for General Washington

fetched. Danny sank down wearily, too, and at once Uncle Benjamin and the children launched into a torrent of questions. Where had the boys been? Why had they been gone so long? How had Gil been hurt? What had happened in Philadelphia? And where was the silver for General Washington?

Sharply Aunt Abigail put an end to the questioning.

"Leave the lads alone until they are rested and fed," she commanded. And she asked Uncle Benjamin to set a kettle of water over the fire so that the boys could have a good warm wash, told Jenifer to go to the room in the attic for dry clothing, suggested to Patsy and Evan that they help Danny take off his shoes, and kneeled down herself beside Gil to pull the wet stocking off his wounded leg.

Already, however, Gil and Danny were fumbling under their jackets and tugging at the money belts which were fastened around their waists. Gil pulled his off first.

"There!" he exclaimed, his eyes shining as he laid the heavy strip of linen in Aunt Abigail's hands. "We couldn't bring the silver, but that's gold—real

Valley Forge Again

gold to help General Washington win the war. Put it away safe, please, until we carry it to him tomorrow."

Danny had taken his belt off by this time, too, and had handed it to Uncle Benjamin. And now there was a new flood of questions. But Aunt Abigail, who had noticed that the boys were shivering, firmly stopped all talk for the time being and asked Uncle Benjamin to lock both belts in his money box.

Before long Gil's leg had been freshly bandaged and both boys were warm and snug in dry clothing. Then, between big mouthfuls of hot mush and milk, they told, bit by bit, the story of their adventures.

Jenifer exclaimed with pleasure when she heard that Ezra had come back to her father's house to look after it. And Patsy's and Evan's eyes grew as big as saucers when Danny described how he and Gil had crossed the ice over the Schuylkill below Gray's Ferry and how Gil had been shot.

"We didn't know whether any more soldiers would chase us or not," Danny said. "Poor Gil couldn't travel very fast with a piece out of his leg, so he gave me his money belt and told me to run. I did run, too, faster than I ever have before, until I came to Mr. Edwards' house. At first Mr. Edwards didn't want to let me in. But when I said 'Lafayette' the way the man in Philadelphia told us to, and explained what had happened, he pushed right past me and went racing down the road to get Gil."

"I was glad to see him, too, because by the time he reached me I was just crawling along," Gil declared, swallowing the last mouthful of his second bowl of mush, and laying down his spoon. "He carried me on his back all the way to his house. And then Mrs. Edwards fixed my leg and made me go to bed and stay there for three days."

"It was kind of her to take such good care of you," Aunt Abigail remarked.

Uncle Benjamin snorted. "Kind!" he exclaimed. "Why, these lads are heroes, Abby. Anybody ought to be glad to help them."

Aunt Abigail smiled. "Heroes or not, they are going to bed this minute," she retorted, pushing her chair back from the table and standing up.

Uncle Benjamin shook his head and caught her around the waist. "Oh, no, they're not!" he exclaimed, sitting her down gently in her chair again. "Look here, old lady, they haven't even told us yet how they got home from Gray's Ferry." He turned to Danny. "Who brought you home?" he asked.

"Mr. Edwards gave us a ride in his farm wagon as far as the Sorrel Horse Inn on the Lancaster Road," Danny replied. "There he found a wagoner he knew who was hauling casks of salt fish to Valley Forge, and he asked him to bring us along."

Gil grinned and made a face. "That was the worst part of the whole journey," he declared. "The fish smelled terrible, and there wasn't any way we could get out of the rain, and the wagon jiggled and jounced until I thought we'd both fall apart."

"Didn't it hurt your leg?" Jenifer asked, looking at her brother as though she never wanted to let him out of her sight again.

Gil nodded. "Yes, it did," he admitted honestly. "But it's better now. And don't fret about it, Jen. I'll soon be able to walk as well as ever." He put his hand on his sister's arm. "Did any letter come from Father while I was gone?" he asked.

Jenifer shook her head and started to reply, but before she could speak Danny had asked his father what had happened to Mr. Thomas Maddock. Then Gil wanted to know if anyone had seen Seth and how Davey's leg was. So the talk turned from one thing to another until Evan had fallen asleep with his head on the table, and even Gil and Danny were yawning. Yet the boys would not go to bed until they had obtained a promise from Uncle Benjamin to let them ride old Peg over to General Washington's headquarters the following morning so that they could deliver the gold they had brought from Philadelphia.

At last Uncle Benjamin helped Gil upstairs. Danny carried Evan to his trundle bed, with Patsy staggering after him, only half-awake. And Aunt Abigail and Jenifer cleared away the supper dishes. Soon all was quiet in the Gardner house and everyone was asleep save Gil, who was so excited at the thought of talking with General Washington the next day that he lay awake until long after the big clock in the kitchen had struck twelve, planning just what he would say and how he would say it.

CHAPTER FIFTEEN

Gil and Danny Call on General Washington

GIL LEANED on his crutch and looked at General Washington and could not say a word.

For the second time the General asked, "Well, my lads, what can I do for you?"

This time he spoke rather hurriedly, for he had had a very busy morning and his desk was piled high with things to which he must attend. Indeed, much as he liked children, he would never have stopped on such a busy day to speak with two boys if it had not been for his wife. Martha Washington herself had brought the boys in to him.

"I found them on the step arguing with the sentry and insisting that they must talk with you," she whispered to her husband. "The lad with the crutch says they have something to give you and

Silver for General Washington

they won't give it to anyone else. Do speak to them for a minute if you can."

And so, to please his good Martha, General Washington was now waiting for the boys, who were standing speechless with awe and excitement before his desk, to tell him why they were there.

It was Danny who spoke first.

"Gil has—has money for you, sir, to help you win the war," he stammered. He nudged his cousin. "Give it to him, Gil," he said.

Silently Gil laid on the General's desk the neat cloth bag made by Aunt Abigail that morning to hold the gold coins, which she had ripped from the travel-worn money belts. General Washington smiled as he unfastened the bag, but his smile changed to an expression of surprise when he poured the coins it contained into a little pile before him.

"This is a very welcome gift," he said quietly, looking at Gil with steady gray eyes. "Before accepting so much money, however, I must know how you came by it."

"Oh, sir!" Gil exclaimed, finding his tongue at last, "my father would want you to have it. Indeed he would. He wrote a letter to my sister and to me before he went away, and told us to do everything we could to help drive King George's soldiers out of the land and to make our country independent. So when one of your soldiers said that you needed hard money to win the war, Danny and I went to

Silver for General Washington

Philadelphia and dug up the silver which was buried in the cellar and sold it and——"

"Just a minute, lad." George Washington's eyes twinkled as he held up a big hand. "You cover so much ground in one breath that I cannot keep pace with you. You say you were in Philadelphia." He leaned forward earnestly. "How long ago?"

"Five days ago, sir," Gil replied, taking care to speak more slowly. "We would have got here sooner, except that near Gray's Ferry a British picket shot me in the leg and I had to wait at Mr. Edwards' house until——"

Again the General interrupted him. Turning to a slim young officer who had just entered the room with a sheaf of papers in his hands, he said, "Colonel Hamilton, will you have the kindness to bring two chairs for these lads? One of them is wounded and we must not keep him standing. Then make ready, if you please, to write down what they have to say, for they have recently come from territory held by the enemy."

With a quick nod Colonel Hamilton placed two chairs near the General's desk and the boys sat down. The colonel provided himself with writing

Gil and Danny Call on Washington

materials and drew up a chair too. At once General Washington began to question Danny and Gil about Philadelphia.

He wanted to know if any new fortifications had been built near the city and where the sentinels were stationed. Gil and Danny were glad now that they had spent so much time roaming around Philadelphia, for they were able to give him much of the information he desired. At last General Washington motioned to the heap of gleaming coins on his desk.

"Will you tell me now just how you obtained this gold which you want to give to help your country?" he questioned, looking gravely from one boy to the other. "I will have to ask you to make your story brief, for there are several people outside waiting to see me."

By this time both Gil and Danny were feeling much more at ease, and Gil was able to tell his story just as he had planned it lying in bed the night before. Only once did General Washington stop him.

"What is your father's name?" he asked.

"It is the same as mine, sir," Gil replied. "Gilbert Emmet."

Silver for General Washington

"Gilbert Emmet," George Washington repeated, rubbing his chin and staring thoughtfully at Gil. Then suddenly his face lighted. "Oh, of course, now I know," he said softly. "Go on."

So Gil, with Danny's help, completed the story of the silver and of how it had been sold. He repeated, as well as he could remember it, the message which the old patriot in Philadelphia had given him, and told quickly of the assistance he and Danny had had from Mr. and Mrs. Edwards.

When he had finished, General Washington nodded slowly. "Colonel," he said, turning to Alexander Hamilton, "this boy's father is, as you know, now in Holland trying to arrange a loan for us. I feel sure that he would be proud of what his son is doing in his absence. Will you therefore be so good as to count this money and make out a receipt for it to Mr. Gilbert Emmet, which I will sign?"

"Holland!" Gil thought, hardly hearing these last words. "Now I know where my father is! Holland!" And bursting with excited questions he started to ask the General how his father was and how much longer he would have to be away.

But already General Washington was standing

up. It seemed to Danny and Gil, who rose also, that his head would touch the ceiling of the low room, he was so tall. Coming around his desk he laid a hand on each boy's shoulder.

"In the name of our country, which we now call the United States of America, I accept this money for which you brave lads have run such risks," he said, looking down at them soberly. "You have done our army and myself a real service. Is there anything now that I can do for you?"

"Oh yes, sir!" Danny blurted out, not giving Gil an opportunity to ask the questions about his father which were on the tip of his tongue. "Please tell my pa that I am old enough to join the army. He says I am too young, but Johnny Geyer is only eleven and he is a drummer boy. I am thirteen and strong for my age."

"I, too, sir," Gil added quickly. "I'd like to fight, too, if I could help to free my country."

Smiling at the boys' eagerness, General Washington shook his head. "Fighting is for men—not for boys," he declared. "And you must remember that fighting alone will not win any war. You lads have already struck a real blow at the enemy by

Silver for General Washington

obtaining money for our soldiers. There will be other ways—many other ways in which you and all the people who must remain at home can help. And when the war is over and our country is independent at last, then it will be your task to aid in building it into a strong, united land."

He turned to Colonel Hamilton. "The receipt, Colonel—is it ready?" he asked.

"Yes, sir," Colonel Hamilton replied, handing his chief a piece of paper and a quill pen which had already been dipped in ink. "It's a tidy sum the boys have brought."

"And badly needed, too," General Washington added. Then, bending over, he signed his name, sanded the paper, folded it, and gave it to Gil.

"Keep this for your father, if you please, and give it to him when he returns," he said.

Gil looked up earnestly into the big man's face. "Please tell me about my father, sir," he begged. "Is he well? When will he be home? Jenifer and I haven't had a letter from him since he went away last September."

"That has been hard for you, I know," General Washington said kindly. "I believe that he is well. I

Gil and Danny Call on Washington

can't tell you when he will be able to return to this country. But I expect to have some news of him, and you should, too, before another month is out."

He shook hands warmly then with each boy, and turned back to his desk. Proudly Gil put the receipt into his greatcoat pocket. He felt happier than he had in many days, as he picked up his hat and crutch and followed Danny through the hall, which was filled with people waiting to see the General.

He said little, however, as he and his cousin mounted old Peg and started the horse toward home. Danny, too, was silent. Both boys' thoughts were on the tall, grave, kindly man whom they had just left, and on his shabby, hungry army.

It was noon when Gil and Danny reached the crossroad where the Connecticut huts stood. The day was warm and several of the soldiers were cooking their dinners of salt fish and rice over outside fires. Gil looked about, hoping to find Seth or one of his other friends among them. But he did not see them, and he dared not stop to look for them, for he and Danny had promised to return to the house as soon as they left the headquarters. The entire family was waiting, of course, to hear about the boys'

Silver for General Washington

meeting with General Washington, and the talk at the dinner table was all of this, and of the news about Mr. Emmet.

Gil, who had hoped that he might borrow old Peg again and ride her back to the Connecticut huts that afternoon, was disappointed when Uncle Benjamin announced after dinner that he was going to harness the horse to the plow to see if she were strong enough to plow up the back field.

The old black mare did so well that for several days thereafter Uncle Benjamin lent her in turn to neighboring farmers whose horses had been stolen by the Hessians or taken over by the American army. This meant that Gil was unable to get about the camp at all until his leg was well enough so that he could walk without pain. Nearly two weeks passed by before he was able to set out on foot in search of Seth, late one Saturday afternoon.

Many things had happened in the camp since the snowy day when Gil and Danny had started out for Philadelphia. Now the snow was gone. Muddy brown meadows were beginning to show tinges of green. Birds, returning from the South, twittered and chirped, searching in vain for trees. But nearly

Gil and Danny Call on Washington

all the trees of Valley Forge had been chopped down to make campfires or to build huts and fortifications.

Ragged soldiers were hard at work strengthening these fortifications, for they knew that the enemy was scarcely twenty miles away and might decide at any minute to attack them. Other ragged soldiers were drilling on the big parade ground, marching and wheeling and shouldering arms, and trying to understand the commands of their new German drillmaster, General Steuben.

Silver for General Washington

When the thirteen American colonies had first decided to liberate themselves from King George's rule, a number of freedom-loving men in Europe had crossed the ocean to help the brave new country in its fight. Chief among the men who had come from France was the tall, blue-eyed, young Lafayette, who had fought gallantly with the American soldiers and had been wounded at the battle on Brandywine Creek. From Poland, Count Pulaski had arrived to lead a band of four hundred horsemen against the redcoats. And the German general, Steuben, had recently come from Prussia to teach the American soldiers how to march and fight together.

Such teaching was badly needed. Farmers, blacksmiths, storekeepers, teachers, students, hunters, and backwoodsmen had enlisted under General Washington to defend their country. They were stout-hearted men, but they had not yet learned that a good army must obey orders quickly and keep its weapons in excellent condition at all times.

General Steuben was shocked to find the American soldiers cooking food over their fires on the points of their bayonets. He was amazed when he

Gil and Danny Call on Washington

learned that they often ignored or disobeyed the commands of their officers. But he was filled with admiration when he saw how courageously and cheerfully they were enduring the hardships of the winter. And he was determined to make them into as fine an army as possible before they should again meet the redcoats in battle.

Day after day he drilled different companies of men, and as Gil now walked past the parade ground which lay across the road from the Gardner house, he could hear him shouting commands in his strange broken English. The boy stopped to watch for a minute while the soldiers in their tattered clothing marched back and forth. Then he went on toward the Connecticut huts. He walked slowly and it was well after five o'clock when he reached the hut where Seth lived. All drilling was over for the day and the men had returned to their little log cabins to rest and to eat their suppers.

The door to Seth's hut was ajar. Gil pushed it open and looked around. He could tell at once that something unusual was afoot, for the plank table had been pulled into the center of the room and set with bark-slab plates and pewter mugs. And Seth

Silver for General Washington

was crouching before the fire roasting a scrawny goose. The old soldier struggled to his feet the minute he saw Gil in the doorway.

"Lord love you, lad, 'tis good to see you," he cried. "Where have you been all this long time?"

"To Philadelphia," Gil replied, his eyes twinkling.

At this, Henry, who was squatting on the floor cracking a little pile of hickory nuts, let out a whoop of laughter. "That's a likely story," he declared, grinning at Gil.

"It's true," Gil protested. "I vow it's true. Look, here's where a British picket shot me."

He pulled up the leg of his breeches to show Henry his wound. Immediately Henry, Caleb, and Tom, as well as three new recruits to the army whom Gil did not know, surrounded him. They all asked questions at once and asked them so quickly that Gil did not know which one to answer first. Seth came to his rescue.

"Leave the lad be," he commanded. "Leave him set down a spell an' rest afore you jumps on him like that." He pushed a stool toward Gil and the boy sat down.

Gil and Danny Call on Washington

"Um, duck!" Gil said, sniffing. "Where in the world did you get it?"

"It ain't duck. It's goose," Seth told him. "You see, we're havin' a bit of celebration for young Davey. He's leavin' us," he said. "Tom here, lucky like, found a wild goose with its wing broke and we've managed to get ourselves some taters that ain't been too badly froze an' with them an' some gravy made from the goose drippin's an' Henry's hickory nuts, it'll be a real feast."

"Where's Davey going?" Gil asked with a sinking feeling in his heart, for he knew that wherever Davey went his violin would go also.

"He's a-goin' to be one of them new Life Guards for General Washington," Seth replied proudly, "an' live in one of them huts behind the General's headquarters." He left his goose to cook, stood up, and brushed off his knees. "Looks like our celebration will be a double one seein' as you're back again," he said kindly. "Kin you tell us now somethin' about your journey?"

So Gil began the story of the trip to Philadelphia. By the time he had finished and had answered all the questions put to him by the men in the hut, the

Silver for General Washington

goose was cooked and Davey had come in. Gil stood up to leave, but Davey and Seth pressed him to stay. Since he had told Aunt Abigail where he was going and knew she would not worry if he were late getting home, he agreed.

"Only I'm not a bit hungry," he declared, realizing as he watched Henry carve the goose that each man would get only a very small portion.

Henry grinned. "All the more for us, then," he said. But he placed a bark plate before Gil with just as much on it as the other plates held and insisted that he take it. The men sat around the fire while they ate and talked about the holiday the camp had been given on St. Patrick's Day when they had all played at Long Bullet, rolling cannon balls to see whose would go the farthest; and then had watched Captain McClane's band of Indian scouts shoot feathered arrows at a little copper coin fifty yards away and hit it almost every time. And they told Gil about the dinner General Steuben had just given for some of his officers.

"There wasn't one man could come to that meal 'lessen his breeches was worn thin enough to have patches on 'em, and what they had to eat wasn't

Gil and Danny Call on Washington

near as good as this," Tom declared, wiping up his last drop of goose gravy with a piece of fire cake.

The meal was soon over and Caleb suggested to Davey that he bring out his violin. "Let's have a little tune," he said. "We'll miss the fiddle sore when you're gone."

Davey chuckled. "More than you'll miss me, I'll warrant," he said, lifting the violin tenderly from its box. He tightened his bow, tuned the strings, and began to play *Yankee Doodle*—a favorite song with all the soldiers. One after another the men began to sing. Other soldiers from nearby huts who had heard the music came in to listen or to add their voices to the chorus. Gil sang too, looking longingly all the while at the violin and yearning to get his hands on it. Perhaps Davey saw his look. At any rate, he stopped after a while and thrust the fiddle at Gil.

"Your turn now, lad," he said. "Give us something lively."

Gil shrank back, unwilling to play before so many strangers. But Henry teased him. "What's wrong, boy? You'd brave the redcoats in Philadelphia and then are afraid of us?"

Silver for General Washington

"Philadelphia!" one of the new recruits exclaimed. "Who's been to Philadelphia?"

"He has!" Seth said with pride, laying an arm across the boy's shoulders. "Tell 'em, Gil."

Again Gil had to tell his story. Again he had to show his wound. The men made much of him and when he had finished, Davey asked him once more to play. So he tucked his own beloved fiddle under his chin, fumbled through a few notes and began a rollicking country dance which his father had taught him. When he had finished he handed the violin back to Davey. "I have to go now," he said. "It's getting late."

"I'll walk along with you a piece, lad," Seth told him. And together the two set out. It was dark, but the stars were bright and the air was mild. Gil thought of his violin as he walked along, wondering if he would ever see it again, and what his father would say when he found that it was gone. Apparently Seth, too, was thinking of the fiddle, for he spoke of it as they neared the Gardner house.

"Since Davey is a-leavin' us, maybe you'll bring your own fiddle to the hut an' play to us a bit now and then," he suggested.

"I can't," Gil said miserably. "I haven't any. The Hessians stole it." Then, afraid that he might be tempted to say more about the theft of his violin, he blurted out a quick "good night."

"Don't come any farther now, Seth. You've a long walk back and I'm almost home," he said, and he started to run, leaving Seth in the middle of the road, staring after him and wondering what had come over the boy.

CHAPTER SIXTEEN

The Army Marches Away

It seemed that spring would never come to Valley Forge, in the year 1778. March was a mild month, full of false promises, warm, and friendly to returning birds and swelling buds. But April blustered in, bringing raw, dismal days, and coating the Schuylkill River again with ice from shore to shore. Yet despite the weather, fifes shrilled and drums beat daily, calling soldiers to the drill grounds.

Under the commands of General Steuben, straggling lines grew straighter, men stepped out more smartly, carried their weapons more proudly, and made themselves ready to give the enemy a good fight when next they met him on the battlefield.

Some of the men had new uniforms now, sent to them by their states, or made, since materials were very scarce, from scarlet and blue cloth captured

The Army Marches Away

from a British ship. And while no one ever had quite enough to eat, everyone was better fed than he had been for many months. Wagon trains, coming from parts of the country which had not been raided and stripped of food, rumbled into camp bringing meat and flour. Most of the soldiers had tasted no vegetables except potatoes during the long winter. Now many of them roamed the fields seeking dandelion and wild mustard greens. Others looked for herbs with which to cure various ailments.

One day when the weather had turned warm again and the dogwood trees were in blossom and the air was sweet with the scent of lilacs, Seth was searching near the river for some elderberry bushes. The bark of these bushes, if burned to charcoal and mixed with fat, made a salve which would, he hoped, heal an old sore on his arm. Gil and Danny were with him.

As they walked along, talking together, they saw three soldiers from the New Hampshire Brigade wading about in the river, looking for mussels. Suddenly one of the New Hampshire men called out excitedly.

"Hey! Look at that!" he shouted. "Something's

Silver for General Washington

wrong with the water! It's all roiled up! Lord save us, it's *fish!*"

And there, leaping and flashing in the sun, struggling to get upstream to spawn, were thousands of big fish.

"They are shad!" Danny cried joyfully. "The shad have come!" And he raced across the fields to his home to get his father's net. His cries, and the

The Army Marches Away

cries of the men wading in the river, attracted many soldiers. Soon the banks of the Schuylkill were crowded with men, who splashed into the water, caught the slippery, wriggling fish in their hands, and tossed them out on the shore.

Farmers living nearby came running with their nets, which they placed across the river near the mouth of Perkiomen Creek. Yelling, shouting, hitting the water with sticks or branches, a hundred soldiers on horseback rode into the stream and drove the shad before them up the Schuylkill River and into the big nets.

Before dark, thousands of fine, fat fish had been taken from the river. For the first time in months every man in Valley Forge had more than he could eat and not a man went hungry to his bunk that night. The next morning the shad were still arriving, and the next day and the next. By the time the run was over, not only had the soldiers had their fill of fish, but hundreds of barrels of rich shad had been salted down to be used at a later day.

As for the Gardners, Aunt Abigail served shad for so many meals that Danny held his nose impolitely whenever he smelled one cooking, and Jeni-

Silver for General Washington

fer, who didn't care much for fish anyway, began to see them in her dreams. However, she was soon too busy to think much about this, for she and Patsy were making May baskets and roaming the woods with Danny and Gil and Evan in search of violets and hepaticas with which to fill them.

The soldiers, too, were getting ready to celebrate the first of May. Like children some of them scoured the forests, looking for tall, straight trees which could be used as Maypoles, one for each regiment. Others stripped the cherry trees of blossoms with which to adorn their hats and those of their friends. Still others laid plans for a big parade.

May Day dawned bright and fair. Midmorning found the men gathering in a long column on the parade ground, shouting and cheering as they fell into line. Meanwhile before each regimental Maypole thirteen soldiers, clad in makeshift costumes of white, each carrying a bow and thirteen arrows, had taken their places. Also before every Maypole had stepped a soldier dressed to look like King Tammany, the Indian chief.

Suddenly thirteen fifers piped shrilly. Thirteen drummers beat their drums, and down the long line

The Army Marches Away

the order came to march. Waving their flower-decked hats and shouting, the men marched gaily from Maypole to Maypole. Villagers came running to see the parade. Wives and children of the soldiers, who had endured the terrible winter in the camp with their husbands and fathers, gathered along the line of march, watching proudly. Back and forth the men marched before the quarters of their generals, cheering and shouting and cutting capers in the warm May sunshine. When finally the parade was over, all the rest of the day was spent in singing, dancing, and games.

Meanwhile, in his headquarters, General Washington was rejoicing over the most welcome piece of news which had come to him in a long time—news which soon spread throughout the entire camp and through the village. Everywhere officers and soldiers, farmers, their wives, and even their children, were talking joyfully about it.

"What's all the turmoil?"

"Haven't you heard? We're getting help from across the seas. France is sending it—shipping clothing and guns and munitions and money. The King of France has signed a treaty of alliance. He will

Silver for General Washington

send soldiers—thousands of them—to help us drive the redcoats and the Hessians from our land."

So the talk ran, and as the news was carried by messenger throughout the colonies, the American people were filled with new hope and encouragement. In Valley Forge General Washington set aside a special day, May sixth, for thanksgiving and celebration. Early on that Wednesday morning Gil and Danny crept from their beds, hastily swallowed a bite of breakfast, and ran off to the parade ground, determined not to miss a moment of the excitement.

It was a day to remember. Joyfully the drums and fifes sounded their call. The men of each brigade fell into their places, straightened their lines, and listened with bowed heads to the solemn prayers of thanksgiving read by their chaplains. Then proudly they marched together down the parade ground toward their Commander in Chief.

Surrounded by trimly dressed French officers, George Washington sat on his big gray horse, erect and smiling, watching his soldiers approach. When they had halted, thirteen ear-splitting cannon shots boomed forth. Raising their muskets the soldiers

The Army Marches Away

fired blank charges into the air and broke into loud cheers. Three cheers for the King of France! And three cheers for the friendly powers of Europe! And three cheers for the United States of America!

Gil grinned at Danny as the last cheer died away. "If the redcoats in Philadelphia don't hear that, they're deaf," he said. And seeing that the men were about to break ranks, he set out at a run for the Connecticut huts, hoping to reach them before Seth and the others returned.

There were extra rations for every soldier that day. Then there were games and races, and finally some of the young officers gave a play. Many people in Valley Forge went to their beds that night with the echoes of the cheers which followed the play still sounding in their ears.

Why the British did not attack the army at Valley Forge during these days of celebration, no one knew. But they did not. Nor did they come during the long, lazy days that followed. Blue skies looked down on men splashing in the waters of the Schuylkill and of Valley Creek, washing away the grime of the terrible winter. The sun shone warmly, chasing away the memories of the winter's cold.

Silver for General Washington

Food grew more plentiful and past hunger was forgotten. The sick gained health and strength. The schoolhouse, no longer needed as a hospital, was turned into a school once more, for soldiers who wanted to learn to read and write.

One lovely evening late in May, when Gil and Danny were returning from Slab Tavern across Valley Creek, where they had been doing an errand for Uncle Benjamin, they stopped near General Washington's headquarters to watch some men playing "rounders." At first they did not recognize the man in shirt sleeves who stood with a bat in his hand, laughing at another man about to toss a ball. Then suddenly Gil pulled Danny's arm excitedly.

"Look!" he exclaimed. "That's General Washington—and without his wig!"

At that very moment the ball was thrown through the air. Swinging his bat, the General hit it with such force that it sailed across the field and dropped into the road where the boys were standing. They scrambled to get it, but it was Gil who laid hands on it first and ran to return it to the General.

"Thank you, lad," General Washington said,

The Army Marches Away

pushing a lock of red hair back from his forehead. Smiling down at Gil he drew his brows together thoughtfully. "Aren't you young Emmet?" he asked.

"Yes, sir," Gil replied, proud that the General should remember his name.

"Did you get your letter?"

"Letter, sir?" Gil asked in surprise.

General Washington nodded. "From your father. One arrived for me today, sent from Holland by way of France and brought here from the coast by messenger. There was one for you, also, which I gave to an orderly to deliver to you. You will no doubt find it at home when you get there."

"Oh, thank you, sir!" Gil exclaimed. And calling to Danny to come along, Gil set off for the Gardner house at a good pace. Jenifer met him at the door with the letter in her hands.

"It's addressed to you," she said. "Do open it quickly." So Gil sat down on the low front step with Jen beside him, broke the seal on his letter, and began to read.

The letter—a long one—had been many months on the way, for the date it bore was December 9,

1777. Mr. Emmet wrote of his rough voyage across the Atlantic, told the children something about the country of Holland, and sent messages to Uncle Benjamin and Aunt Abigail. Then he reminded Gil to practice daily on his violin, said he hoped that Jenifer would study diligently while he was away, and signed himself "Your loving Father."

When Gil had finished the letter and he and Jen had talked it over, Jenifer took it from him and slowly read over parts of it again. Then, in answer to Patsy's call to supper, she and her brother went into the house. The next morning, as soon as he had finished his chores, Gil set out for the Connecticut huts to tell Seth that he had heard at last from his father. He found the old soldier behind the hut with Tom and Caleb. Tom was shaving Caleb, who was perched on a three-legged stool brought from the hut, and Seth was cooking a strange-looking mixture of dogwood leaves, bark, and water, over a small fire.

" 'Tis for my hair," Seth explained rather sheepishly, when Gil asked him what was in the pot. "Caleb, here, says it will make it grow thick as grass, an' the good Lord knows so much of mine came

The Army Marches Away

a-fallin' out last winter that I can't make a queue no thicker than a bit of string." He gave the mixture a stir with a long stick and sat down on the ground with his arms wrapped around his knees, looking up at Gil.

"You seem kind of pert this mornin', young feller," he said. "What's come over you?"

Gil grinned. "I've had a letter from my father," he replied, squatting on the ground beside Seth. And he told the men about his letter from Holland.

Tom scraped the razor over Caleb's chin. "You ain't the only one with news," he drawled. "There's a story flyin' 'round the camp that the British are fixin' to move out of Philadelphiay. I wouldn't wonder if we'd be settin' out after 'em afore long."

"Oh!" Gil remarked dully, realizing suddenly how much he would miss his friends when they had left. "How soon will you be going?"

Seth spat out a piece of grass on which he had been chewing. "I don't know," he replied. "Young Davey was here last night, a-struttin' 'round like a rooster in his new uniform, an' he says the Life Guards at headquarters are a-talkin' 'bout some time maybe in a day or two." He stood up and stirred the brew in the pot again. "I hope we won't have to wait no longer than that," he declared. "I'm just a-hankerin' for General Washington to lead us agin the redcoats in a real good fight."

Seth was not the only soldier in Valley Forge longing for action. All through the encampment men were restless and eager to move on. At headquarters General Washington waited anxiously for reports from the spies whom he had placed in and near Philadelphia. He knew that the British were preparing to evacuate the city. But he did not know where they were intending to go, or at what time.

If they should strike out for New York he planned to overtake them with his army in northern New Jersey, and to attack them there. So he issued orders that wagons should be loaded with military stores and that the officers and men should hold themselves ready to leave on short notice.

Mrs. Washington had already bade good-by to her husband and friends and set out in the big family coach for Mount Vernon. Other officers' wives, who did not intend to accompany their husbands on the march, had packed up their children and possessions and started for their homes.

The Army Marches Away

Tensely the men waited for news from Philadelphia. There was such an air of expectancy everywhere that Gil and Danny were afraid to go to bed each night for fear the soldiers might leave before daybreak and they should not see them depart. The boys spent every possible minute now roaming around the encampment, or visiting with Seth and the others. Indeed they stayed at the hut so late on one evening in mid-June that Gil almost missed a very welcome visitor.

It was almost dark and the first stars were shining when he and Danny sauntered up the road. Turning into the path leading to the Gardner house, they saw Aunt Abigail standing in the open doorway with the girls and Evan peering around her skirts, and something which looked very much like one of the neighbors' babies in her arms. She was talking with a soldier whose back was partly turned to the road.

"Thank you kindly, ma'am," Gil and Danny heard the soldier say. Then he swung around on his heel and started down the steps. Gil grinned when he saw that the caller was Davey, for he thought the young soldier had come to say good-by, and per-

Silver for General Washington

haps to show off his new uniform. But the boy's heart skipped a beat when Davey turned, took the bundle from Aunt Abigail's arms, and laid it in his own.

"It's that violin I found," Davey told him, pulling aside the flannel in which the instrument was wrapped. "A Life Guard for General Washington doesn't have much time for fiddling, I've discovered, and anyway I'm sore afraid that it will get hurt when we're on the march. So it's yours if you want it."

"Want it?" Gil's voice was choked. For a moment he could hardly speak. Then, stroking the fiddle lovingly, he said, "I'll—I'll keep it for you safe until the war is over."

Davey shook his head. "I'll not need it again, lad," he said. "My own fiddle waits at home for me. Just remember this. Men fight better if they—well, if they know there's music and things like that waiting for them when they come home. So practice hard until you've learned to play the very best you can."

"I will, oh, indeed I will," Gil promised happily. And then he called good-by, for the young soldier

The Army Marches Away

—as if he felt that he had said too much—had already started away.

"Good night to you all," Davey called back and was off down the road.

The boys had no chance to speak with him again, for the following morning a messenger came galloping into the camp, his face red, his hair disheveled, his horse winded. The British were moving! They were leaving Philadelphia! They were loading their cannon on boats and crossing the Delaware! They were marching toward New York!

At once General Washington gave his orders. Drums were sounded. Men came running from wherever they were to their regimental huts. Horses were brought in from the pastures. Last-minute packing was done. Lines were formed. There was no time for farewells.

Sharply the command rang out, "Brigades forward!" Muskets were shouldered. Fifes screamed. Drums beat. And the soldiers of Valley Forge began to march.

Villagers came streaming from their houses, lining the roads, and running to General Sullivan's bridge over which the army must pass. They

Silver for General Washington

shouted to the men they knew, calling out last messages and good-bys. Uncle Benjamin, Aunt Abigail, Gil, Danny, Jenifer, Patsy, and Evan were there with all the rest, standing close to the bridge, cheering and craning their necks to see everything which was going on.

There rode General Washington, proudly erect on his big horse, and behind him came his officers and men. Horses pranced. Flags flew. Bayonets gleamed in the sun. There seemed to be no end to the noisy shrilling of fifes and the persistent beating of drums—no end to the long, long column of marching soldiers.

What did it matter that only a part of them wore uniforms, and that these uniforms were of various cuts—and colors: browns and grays and reds and blues? Most of the men had shoes. All of the men had muskets. No longer in their minds were they soldiers from thirteen different states, suspicious and quarreling. Now they were soldiers of the United States of America, bound together with one aim—to win liberty and independence for their country. To those who watched it seemed impossible that this smartly stepping, well-drilled army

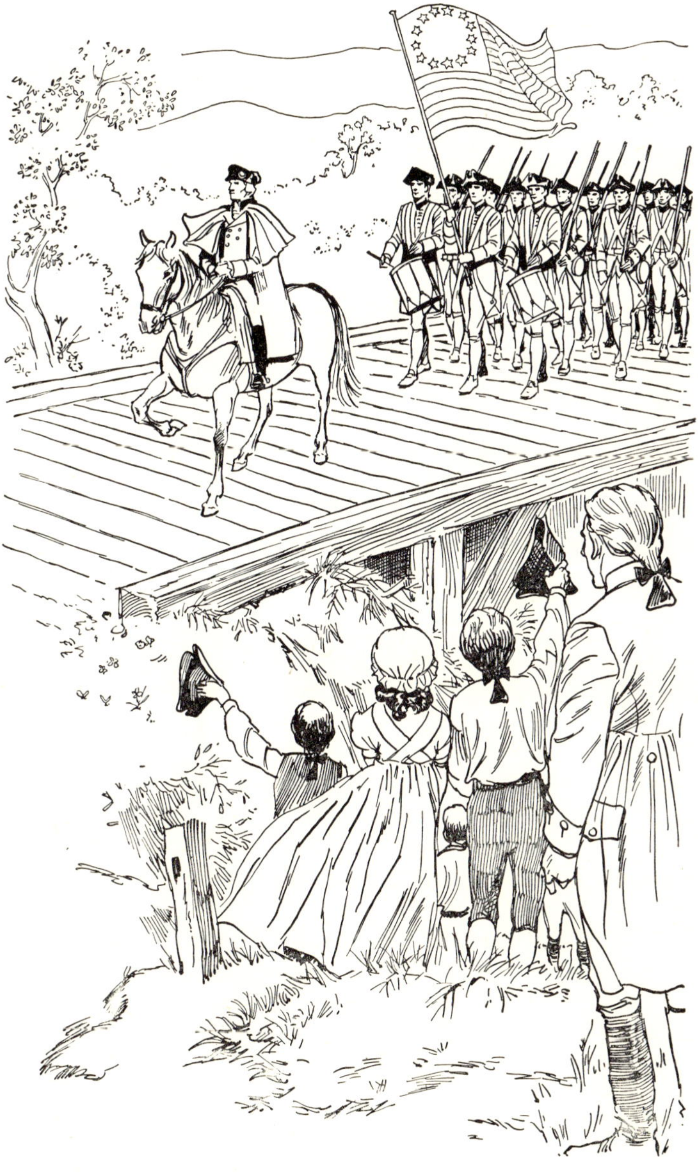

could be the same body of men which had stumbled —broken, ragged, and starving—into Valley Forge just six months earlier.

"It's a miracle—that's what it is," Uncle Benjamin leaned over to say in Aunt Abigail's ear. "A miracle! There's no army in the world that can beat men who have lived through such a winter and can now march away like that."

Aunt Abigail nodded proudly. Then she gave a start, for Gil, who was standing at her side, had spied Seth in the ranks now passing and was shrieking the soldier's name.

"Seth! Oh, Seth!" Gil shouted, his voice shrill and high as he tried to make himself heard above the noise of tramping feet. "Good-by, Seth. Good-by!"

The old soldier turned and grinned and waved his hat.

"Good-by, lad," he shouted. "We're off to lick the redcoats!"

Straightening his musket, which had slipped a little on his shoulder, he marched proudly on. Somewhere in the ranks a man started a song. One after another the soldiers took it up. Their voices were

The Army Marches Away

loud and strong and the words came clearly to the ears of all the listening villagers.

> *"Come, join hand in hand,*
> *Brave Americans all;*
> *And rouse your whole band*
> *At Liberty's call."*

On came the men, singing, in a never ending column. Many people, weary at last of watching them march by, went away. But the Gardners, with Gil and Jenifer, remained until the sun was low in the sky and the last wagon full of military supplies had rumbled over the bridge. Then Uncle Benjamin rose from the grass where they had been sitting and helped Aunt Abigail to her feet.

"Come," he said to the children. "We who remain behind must work harder now than ever before, for our America." And, slipping his arm through Aunt Abigail's, he led the way toward home.

About the Author

Enid La Monte Meadowcroft, the distinguished author of historical fiction and nonfiction books for boys and girls, began to write when she was eleven years old. Her first stories were published in her own newspaper. Since then she has written twenty books for children.

Her other activities have included teaching in both the East and West, traveling throughout the United States and Europe, and keeping house. She has also acted as the supervising editor of a series of biographies.

Miss Meadowcroft was born in New York City, but spent most of her childhood in Cranford, New Jersey. Her home is now in the beautiful Berkshire foothills of Connecticut. She likes dogs, gardening, swimming, and days spent out of doors. She also enjoys reading, music, and American history. And, of course, children!

Her books are popular because, as a seventh grader in Brookline, Massachusetts, once said, "History is okay if it is exciting, like *Silver for General Washington* by Enid La Monte Meadowcroft!"

In addition to the many books, diaries, letters, and articles consulted in writing this story, the author is especially indebted to the cooperation of Mr. Gilbert S. Jones, Executive Secretary of the Valley Forge Park Commission, for furnishing additional helpful data.